MY LORD,
He Calls Me

—— STORIES OF FAITH BY ——
BLACK AMERICAN LATTER-DAY SAINTS

MY LORD, *He Calls Me*

—— STORIES OF FAITH BY ——

BLACK AMERICAN LATTER-DAY SAINTS

ALICE FAULKNER BURCH, GENERAL EDITOR

DESERET BOOK

Salt Lake City, Utah

© 2022 Deseret Book Company

All rights reserved. No part of this book may be reproduced in any form or by any means without permission in writing from the publisher, Deseret Book Company, at permissions@deseretbook.com. This work is not an official publication of The Church of Jesus Christ of Latter-day Saints. The views expressed herein are the responsibility of the authors and do not necessarily represent the position of the Church or of Deseret Book Company.

Deseret Book is a registered trademark of Deseret Book Company.

Visit us at deseretbook.com

Library of Congress Cataloging-in-Publication Data

CIP on file

ISBN 978-1-63993-029-6

Printed in the United States of America
Lake Book Manufacturing, Inc., Melrose Park, IL

10 9 8 7 6 5 4 3 2 1

*This book is dedicated to the Black American First Pioneers
of The Church of Jesus Christ of Latter-day Saints,
whose Faith, Persistence, Perseverance, and Love of God
and Jesus Christ have been our Counsel, Strength,
and Soft Place to Fall when we've needed rest.
We remember. We honor. We celebrate.
With gratitude to God who saw you along the Path . . .*

*Thank you,
Your Spiritual Descendants*

The main title and section titles of this work are from the Negro spiritual "Steal Away to Jesus." Weaving the lyrics of the song throughout these essays is one way of sharing Black American culture with our readers and expressing our heritage of faith and resilience. This song was composed by Wallace Willis, who was enslaved, sometime before 1862. It was popularized by the general public when the famous Jubilee Singers of Fisk University in Nashville performed it on a tour during 1871.[1] Since then, many popular singers have recorded it. In 2018, two members of The Church of Jesus Christ of Latter-day Saints recorded it, renewing it for a whole new audience and generation.[2]

With a soothing melody that reaffirms faith, the song simultaneously juxtaposes our mortality and eternal nature while carrying symbolism from the days of enslavement and coded messages understood only by our enslaved Ancestors.

> *Steal away. Steal away.*
> *Steal away to Jesus.*
> *Steal away. Steal away home.*
> *I ain't got long to stay here.*
>
> *My Lord, He calls me.*
> *He calls me by the thunder.*
> *The trumpet sounds within my soul:*
> *I ain't got long to stay here.*

---

1. See G. D. Pike, *The Jubilee Singers and Their Campaign for Twenty Thousand Dollars* (Boston: Lee and Shepard, 1873).
2. See Latter-day Saints Camlyn Giddins and Yahosh Bonner sing this spiritual at https://www.youtube.com/watch?v=czX2JUbbN9w.

Green trees are bendin'.
Poor sinners stand a-tremblin'.
The trumpet sounds within my soul:
I ain't got long to stay here.

My Lord, He calls me.
He calls me by the light'n.
The trumpet sounds within my soul:
I ain't got long to stay here.

CONTENTS

Introduction: "For the Body Is Not One Member, but Many" 1

PART I: "HE CALLS ME BY THE THUNDER"
STANDING CONFIDENTLY IN OUR BLACKNESS

This Body of Color: Four Simple Words 11
   Lita Little Giddins

Our Road Trip to Jesus 18
   Hayley and Millie Fletcher

One Seeking to Know and Learn 24
   Abner Leonard Howell (1878–1966)

Staunch Members of This Religion 29
   Mary Lucille Perkins Bankhead (1902–1994)

Poem: This Body of Being 31

"I, Too, Am Part of God's Plan" 32
   Tayler Jolley

The Path We Take—Do I Belong? 36
   Gloria Talley Wilkinson

In the Same Manner 42
   Eugene Orr

PART II: "GREEN TREES ARE BENDING"
FOLLOWING WHERE THE HOLY SPIRIT LEADS

Slain in the Spirit 57
   Rodric Anthony Johnson

CONTENTS

"As a Mother in Israel, Thou Shalt Be
    Known among the People" 66
    Jane Elizabeth Manning James (1821–1908)

Gifts of God 73
    Alice Faulkner Burch

Spiritual Learning and Social Belonging 79
    Jermaine Sullivan

Spiritually Locked and Loaded 84
    Rah Freestone

Poem: When Truth First Spoke to Me 90

Searching for My Heavenly Father's Church 92
    Pepper McCoy

Born of Goodly Parents 100
    Wayne Lee

Where Heavenly Father Led Me 103
    Esther M. Branch

Hosanna! Hosanna! 109
    Elizabeth "Bessie" Ritchie Rogers (1884–1970)

The Answer? The Plan of Salvation 112
    Sherri Camp

God Wanted Me in This Church 118
    Stuart Scott

I Knew It Was True 124
    Norma Banks

PART III: "STEAL AWAY TO JESUS"
FINDING FAITH IN TRIALS AND PRESSING FORWARD

What *Are* You? 131
    Anonymous

From Tabernacle to Temple 136
    Kayla Wyatt

CONTENTS

Not Necessarily Fair 141
   Kevin Flowers

Poem: Without 148

I Thought the Gospel Was Free for
   Anyone That Wanted to Hear It 149
   Marie Benjamin Graves (1878–1930)

Identity and Priority 152
   Parker M. Jolley

The Family with the Black Kids 158
   Abigail Hansen

Poem: Jesus Understands Me Black 162

Is That Still a Thing? 164
   Robert S. Burch Jr.

PART IV: "THE TRUMPET SOUNDS WITHIN MY SOUL"
TESTIMONIES OF TRUTH

Nothing Small in the Kingdom of God 173
   Samuel Davidson Chambers (1831–1929)

Learning the Gospel as a Young Woman 180
   Tianna Jolley

Heritage and Legacy 186
   J. Tekulvē Jackson-Vann

I Know the Work Is of God 190
   John Wesley Harmon Jr. (1881–1940)

Poem: Testimony of an Aged Ancestor on
   Being Banned from the Holy Priesthood 192

The Bicycle Trip 194
   Randy Cutliff and Denise Silva

The Gospel Is Here on Earth 200
   Frances Ann Stewart Hood (1832–1910)

CONTENTS

I Found a Brother 201
   Earl Joseph Hunter Jr.

Poured from the Hand of God 207
   Randall Silas

Creative Narrative: I **Know** the Voice of My Jesus 210

Tuning My Heart to My Ancestors 216
   Kinnith E. Holloway

Acknowledgments 220

Further Reading 222

Sources and Credits 224

INTRODUCTION

"FOR THE BODY IS NOT ONE MEMBER, BUT MANY"

My Lord, He calls me. These words, sung as part of the early Black American spiritual "Steal Away to Jesus," are an apt representation of the testimonies and experiences found in this book. Written by Black American Latter-day Saints, the essays in this collection profess deep faith in Christ, provide inspirational stories on being led by the Holy Spirit, and offer sacred truths on maintaining faith while overcoming challenges, including racism. This book shares a small view of Black American life in The Church of Jesus Christ of Latter-day Saints, covering the experiences of members from the earliest days that their words could be found to now, demonstrating that from the beginning of the Restoration, Black Americans have responded to the call of the Lord to gather into His Church.

The collection was compiled for many purposes: it is meant to strengthen and aid the Black American Latter-day Saint community as well as educate other members of the Church who want to better understand the experiences of Black American Latter-day Saints. These stories and testimonies are also meant to help Latter-day Saints understand what our Church leaders continue to teach about the sin of racism and removing racist attitudes and behaviors from our congregations. President Russell M. Nelson recently stated, "The Creator of us all calls on each of us to abandon attitudes of prejudice against any group of God's children. Any of us who has prejudice toward another race needs to repent!"[1] Ultimately, the hope of this book is to help *all* Church members become united through better understanding one another.

---

1. Russell M. Nelson, "We Are All Children of God," May 25, 2021, https://www.churchofjesuschrist.org/inspiration/we-are-all-children-of-god?lang=eng.

Our Savior commanded, "I say unto you, be one; and if ye are not one ye are not mine" (Doctrine and Covenants 38:27).

CONTRIBUTORS TO THIS VOLUME

The contributors to this book are diverse—of various places, ages, and eras. The places they are from include Alabama, Georgia, Mississippi, Utah, Kansas, Virginia, and Ontario, Canada. Our oldest contributor is seventy-six years old, and our youngest is thirteen. Nine of the testimonies and life stories in this book are from our Ancestors; eight are from some of the earliest Black American Latter-day Saints of whose words we have record. Because of the wide diversity of our contributors, their experiences in the Church are also varied.

Many of our Ancestors, for instance, were members of the Church when slavery was still a legal institution in the United States. Racism and discrimination were widespread and largely accepted by society, but the priesthood, which was restored in 1829, did not exclude any specific race or ethnicity during Joseph Smith's lifetime.[2] In 1852, under President Brigham Young, what Latter-day Saints commonly refer to as the "priesthood ban" was first instituted, excluding those of Black African heritage from priesthood ordination and higher temple ordinances. Black American men were no longer ordained to the priesthood, and the priesthood of those few who had already been ordained was not recognized or accepted by the Church. Black American men and women were not permitted to receive their higher ordinances in the temple, which included receiving the endowment and being sealed to their spouses, even if the spouse was White American.

Several of our contributors share their experiences of finding the gospel during this period of over one hundred years when Black

---

2. "There is no reliable evidence that any black men were denied the priesthood during Joseph Smith's lifetime" ("Race and the Priesthood," Gospel Topics Essays, The Church of Jesus Christ of Latter-day Saints, https://www.churchofjesuschrist.org/study/manual/gospel-topics-essays/race-and-the-priesthood?lang=eng).

INTRODUCTION

Americans could not receive all ordinances and when racist beliefs and attitudes were more accepted than they are now. In 1978, the ban was lifted by a revelation received by President Spencer W. Kimball. Official Declaration 2 reflects this revelation and is now canonized as scripture in the Church. In the mainstream of the Black American community, we refer to this as the restoration of the priesthood as Brother Joseph originally received it.

Many of our younger contributors were "born into the Church" and were not alive when the revelation on the priesthood was given in 1978. Yet, as several of them attest, many Latter-day Saints still "advanced many theories to explain the priesthood and temple restrictions."[3] And although "none of these explanations is accepted today as the official doctrine of the Church" and our leaders have stated that they "unequivocally condemn all racism, past and present, in any form,"[4] hurtful and rude words and actions still come from some members of the Church. Many of our contributors share their experiences of holding to the truth and the witness of the Holy Spirit as they have navigated these challenges.

Though our contributors' lives are varied, they are all united by a common thread of faith in the Lord. Black American lives are shadowed—both religiously and nonreligiously—by deep and abiding faith in Jesus Christ that has produced miracles and many gifts of the Spirit in our lives and those of our family and friends, granted by our compassionate God. Our shared faith has also created tight community ties, which have aided our survival and strengthened us since the days our Ancestors were enslaved. When our people were legally forbidden to gather, spirituality existed without formal religion. And that spirituality has remained with us as we eventually

---

3. "Race and the Priesthood," Gospel Topics Essays, The Church of Jesus Christ of Latter-day Saints, https://www.churchofjesuschrist.org/study/manual/gospel-topics-essays/race-and-the-priesthood?lang=eng.
4. "Race and the Priesthood," Gospel Topics Essays.

joined organized religions, including The Church of Jesus Christ of Latter-day Saints. As evidenced by the stories found in these pages, this resilient spirituality and faith has been a part of Black American lives throughout history.

As you review this work, you might ask, "Why aren't there *more* stories told by the early Black American members?" or, "Why not do an entire book in *only* the words of early Black American members?" Sadly, while it is easy to find a pile of direct quotes and even long entries from journals of early White American members of the Church, there is a dearth of actual verbiage from early Black American members. This is likely due to several reasons: (1) Black Americans weren't valued as much as White Americans during the early days of the Church, and so their words were not captured as often; (2) because of laws based on racist attitudes and practices, most Black Americans could not write; (3) records of their words may exist but in private collections that we are currently unaware of; and (4) since the words of Black Americans have historically been undervalued, their papers and documents were not preserved. As research continues to be done by interested and invested Latter-day Saint historians and researchers—such as Ardis Parshall, Amy Thiriot, and Paul Reeve— we hope one day to enjoy the experience of savoring the words of many more early Black American Latter-day Saints.[5] Meanwhile, we treasure what we *do* have and what continues to be found.[6] Regardless of how much we have, I, like other Black American members, feel a bond to each of these individuals and think of them as our "Spiritual Ancestors."

---

5. To explore what we *do* know of early Black Latter-day Saints, we invite you to visit the "Century of Black Mormons" database, hosted by the University of Utah: https://exhibits.lib.utah.edu/s/century-of-black-mormons/page/welcome.
6. For example, a newly discovered "vault" of personal history was recently discovered and led to a new entry into the online database "Century of Black Mormons": that of Elizabeth ("Bessie") Ritchie Rogers, who had a stack of books taller than she is filled with her family history!

INTRODUCTION

ONE BODY IN CHRIST

As you hear the different voices in this book, you will see two profound truths, which hold true for all people: First, Black Americans are not monolithic. Seeing or speaking to one Black American is *not* seeing or speaking to every Black American. Our commonalities and differences are all tied to our individual culture—how we grew up living it and how we live it now.

Second, though Black Americans are all different, we are tied together by a unique culture. This culture, which includes our mannerisms, language, fashion, ancestry, and history, cumulatively differs from that of other People of Color of the African Diaspora. Every author in this book was raised in the United States of America, and most have a lineage connected to slavery. That era forced our Ancestors to create a culture that brought together those from varying parts of Africa, allowing them to unite, form a family, speak to one another, and find comfort in the misery of enslavement. That culture is our heritage and, with some changes along the way, has been passed down through the generations.

The deep reality tied to these two truths is that the strength of the body of the Church lies in our differences in ethnicity, culture, and race. Comparing members of the Church to the body of Christ, the Apostle Paul said to the Corinthians, "For as the body is one, and hath many members, and all the members of that one body, being many, are one body: so also is Christ" (1 Corinthians 12:12). Our differences and unique perspectives are critical to our strength as a people: "And the eye cannot say unto the hand, I have no need for thee: nor again the head to the feet, I have no need of you" (v. 21). For this reason, it is vital that we embrace our differences and behold in them the beauty that God instilled for *all* of us to be blessed.

Verse 23 of 1 Corinthians 12 enunciates very well the spiritual reason for this compilation: "And those members of the body, which we think to be less honourable, upon these we bestow more abundant honour; and our uncomely parts have more abundant comeliness." Unfortunately, Black Latter-day Saints have often been seen as "less honourable," or lesser than, among our own brothers and sisters in the gospel. Racist attitudes and beliefs have often made our going in the Church difficult, and as a result *we—all of us, every* member of the Church—have thereby suffered and been harmed.

Racism affects not just Black Americans. It affects EVERY American regardless of ethnicity or race—whether they're the ones perpetuating the racism, observing it happen, or neither. By coming together into the restored gospel, we have the ability to create a "oneness" and "unity," which Jesus commands us to have (see Doctrine and Covenants 38:27). What continues to stand in our way, however, is misunderstanding the difference between White American culture and the actual gospel of Jesus Christ in our congregations.

This isn't unique or exclusive to The Church of Jesus Christ of Latter-day Saints. Every organized church that has existed for a long period has experienced the same difficulties that come with age and multigenerational membership. For instance, we see Apostles in the New Testament correcting false traditions that had been passed down (see Acts 15 for one example). And in the Book of Mormon, Alma, in his position as Church leader, repeatedly "regulated" the Church in his day (see Mosiah 26:37; Alma 6; and Alma 45:21). Likewise, in the early days of the restored Church, the Prophet Joseph Smith received clear instructions that he and the current Apostles and all subsequent leaders were also to regulate the Church on a consistent basis, in part to root out false teachings (see Doctrine and Covenants 107:33). Although our prophet, apostles, and other Church leaders may speak to this difference between gospel and culture, the traditions and habits that we create as people can still come together and confuse what is the actual gospel of Jesus Christ. The responsibility to make the much-needed change still resides with each individual member.

INTRODUCTION

God has told us to be one, and if we are not one, we are not His. This commandment is not only for one specific group of people—it is for every person, regardless of skin shade, ethnicity, and culture. Becoming "one" and creating unity requires *connection*, and racism destroys our ability to connect with one another. Our hope is that this book will help put in place that vital connection; by reading of our experiences, testimonies, and the feelings of our heart through narrative and poetry, our brothers and sisters of other ethnicities and races have the opportunity to understand, empathize, and become better acquainted with our culture, with our lives as Latter-day Saints, and with us as a people—Black American "members of the body" of Christ.

"HE CALLS ME BY THE THUNDER"

STANDING CONFIDENTLY IN OUR BLACKNESS

"It is because of those things which had transpired, those things which decades ago were less than a dream, that today I harbor magnificent hopes for our future."

—*Darius Gray, founding member and second Genesis Group President*
Born 1945; baptized 1964

THIS BODY OF COLOR: FOUR SIMPLE WORDS

LITA LITTLE GIDDINS

Lita Little Giddins is a seeker of opportunities to improve the condition and climate of the world in every space she enters. She has a master's degree in social work with an emphasis in expressive arts therapy from Brigham Young University and an associate's degree in fine arts from Citrus College in California. Lita lives in Utah, where she is the Coordinator of Diversity, Collaboration, and Inclusion at BYU.

"I don't see color." I hear a lot of uncomfortable and often hurtful statements in the Church community and in my line of work. Some said to me directly. But when I heard a member make this comment recently, despite hearing it multiple times before, it struck a deeper nerve—the spiritual nerve that sees, hears, and feels beyond oneself. The words kept playing over in my mind: "I don't see color." We come to recognize these four basic words when we first begin to learn how to read. When we are young, we're taught what each of them mean, how to use them. As we grow older, the placement of these four simple words when spoken in a sentence becomes more complex.

I found myself asking questions attached to these four simple words for weeks. If a person chooses to not *see* color, why is that? What does that even mean? Because, you see, when I was a young Black girl growing up in Southern California, I didn't want to see my color either. Positive ethnic representations were rarely seen, leaving me with a feeling that something must be wrong with being Black. Ironically, it wasn't until after I was baptized a member of The Church of Jesus Christ of Latter-day Saints, a predominantly White organization at the time, that I began to gain a better, clearer understanding of who I was—and what I was—as a Black female disciple of Jesus Christ.

Since becoming a member of the Church, I feel a tremendous amount of spiritual groundedness and gratitude for being covered in this body of color. It possesses a divine plan and purpose. Without doubt or hesitation, I claim and embrace the full breadth and depth of it. The following poem is a testament to how I feel about Blackness.

SACRED

It has always been this way.
Sacred.
Recognizing. Acknowledging. Accessing its Power.
Adhering to an Eternal Law.
Expecting.
Commanding fair judgment and Equity.
Accepting responsibility for the position of *The Sacred.*
Bearing the weight of everything placed upon
The Sacred.
Laws of man distort, ignore, demean what has been received
In Sacredness.
Believing It is less for use. Not human for use. Servile for use.
Trampled upon and discarded for their use.
Truth;
Conspired falsehoods to mislead, to deceive, and to oppress for
fear of becoming less.
Truth;
It will fulfill its Divine use, never forgetting what has been placed

within *So Sacredly*.
It has always been this way.
Sacred.

I have come a long way from how I used to think and feel about being Black. How I stand in my body now is empowering and faith promoting. Acknowledging my Blackness and standing confidently in my Blackness keeps me intimately connected to my God and is vital to my existence as I continue to learn its positionality in God's plan. In contrast, I wonder, how does choosing to not see color serve the individual? Perhaps deeper meaning can be found in Jesus giving sight to the blind. Could it be part of our very existence, our purpose, and our covenant is to see, in fullness, the sacredness of one another? Pondering such questions proved to serve me well when one day this important question came to mind: "Does Jesus see color?"

While reflecting on this question, my spiritual nerve was nurtured, and I felt faith, truth, and purpose coursing throughout my body with greater strength and conviction.

Let me explain why.

In the Book of Mormon, the prophet Nephi testifies, "The Lord esteemeth all flesh in one" (1 Nephi 17:35). To me that means the diversity of flesh is highly valued, is something God cares about and invites us to be aware of. We live in a society where groups with varying types of "flesh" are highly marginalized. Our Savior was born into and lived in a similar environment. But He came to this earth with a divinely centered mission: to destigmatize traditions and systems embedded within longstanding cultural norms of exclusion throughout the community. Many were

Acknowledging my Blackness and standing confidently in my Blackness keeps me intimately connected to my God and is vital to my existence as I continue to learn its positionality in God's plan.

affected among the stigmatized, including the Samaritans, the lepers, and those metaphorically viewed as "lepers" by those who chose to not see. In truth and clarity, Nephi taught, *"He denieth none that come unto him, black and white"* (2 Nephi 26:33; emphasis added). When one chooses to not see color, I believe a vital part of that person is being denied.

Perhaps this is one of the reasons the prophet Jacob pleads, "Wherefore, a commandment I give unto you, . . . that ye revile no more against [people of color] because of the darkness of their skins" (Jacob 3:9).[1]

These are some of the "plain and . . . precious" things Jesus taught (1 Nephi 14:23). And yet, in His continual efforts to destigmatize societal mindsets at large, the Savior Himself became socially stigmatized, which eventually led to His fated death.

Do we see this part of Jesus? That He was persecuted, dismissed, afflicted, mocked as "King of the Jews" for His race and ethnicity, while hanging from a cross?

I believe the lives lost at the hands of those who view the worth of a person based solely on the color of their skin are intimately understood by the Redeemer because He can "see as they are seen, and know as they are known."

With so many Black lives being taken, often "lepered," esteemed as less, I believe the lives lost at the hands of those who view the worth of a person based solely on the color of their skin are intimately understood by the Redeemer because He can "see as they are seen, and know as they are known" (Doctrine and Covenants 76:94).

---

1. The full verse reads, "Wherefore, a commandment I give unto you, which is the word of God, that ye revile no more against them because of the darkness of their skins; neither shall ye revile against them because of their filthiness; but ye shall remember your own filthiness, and remember that their filthiness came because of their fathers."

THIS BODY OF COLOR: FOUR SIMPLE WORDS

Another nurturing scripture is found in the New Testament—John 9:6. It is the story of the man born blind who was healed. His worth, along with that of his parents, was questioned because of the simple fact that he was born blind. Everyone chose to *see* that part of him.

What moves my soul is how the Savior restored the man's sight. The passage reads: "Master, who did sin, this man, or his parents . . . ? Jesus answered, Neither . . . : but that the works of God should be made manifest in him. . . . When he had thus spoken, he spat on the ground, and made clay [of color] of the spittle, and he anointed the eyes of the blind man with the clay. . . . He went his way therefore, and washed, and came seeing" (John 9:2–3, 6–7).[2]

> *It is written that the Light of Jesus is in* all *things and through* all *things. That includes me. He is in and through my Blackness.*

In a sense, I view myself as clay of color. My desire is to be used by God to invite others who choose to not see to wash their eyes and come seeing. To absolutely see my color, please. Then to take the next step to see beyond, to see more because my Blackness is what adds and gives meaning and purpose to the "more."

I feel an absence of Deity when confronted with reminders that the color of my skin is a problem for some people. It is written that the Light of Jesus is in *all* things and through *all* things (see Doctrine and Covenants 88:6). That includes me. He is in and through my Blackness.

I proposed a question at the beginning: "Does Jesus see color?" Four simple words on their own, but they are packed with plainness and truth when positioned in this query in anticipation of the

---

2. Clay, by definition is made of color. It is "a stiff, sticky fine-grained earth, typically yellow, red, or bluish-gray in color and often forming an impermeable layer in the soil. It can be molded when wet, and is dried and baked to make bricks, pottery, and ceramics." Google Online Dictionary, s.v. "clay."

response. The answer is a resounding *yes*! Every time I approach the scriptures, I feel Jesus looking at this body of color in fullness and my soul looks back, reaffirmed. And since Jesus is in and through all things—the Great Seer of All Flesh, the Repairer of All Injustices—with four simple words, I invite you to consider this. Whenever you see a body of color, do you see Jesus?

THIS BODY OF COLOR (FOUR SIMPLE WORDS)

Earth-toned, stemming from Earth's soil, enriched with Earth's nutrients for the inhabitant's health and wealth;

Mother Earthed is This Body of Color.

Embedded deep within layers of crust, mantle and core dating beyond the age of its sphere is *This Body of Color.*

Blended, composed; a composite of fragmented tones that sustains healing minerals is *This Body of Color.*

Visible distinctions of resilience not relegated to positions of inferiority and neutrality is *This Body of Color.*

Incapable of imperception in determination, perseverance and abundant hope within the history of soil is *This Body of Color.*

No disfavor was born on the plot of land when the Son of Man atoned in *His Body of Color.*

No apologies were uttered or avowed in that place when bleeding flesh quenched the thirsty Earth from *His Body of Color.*

Skin for skin, emboldened with infinite purpose and vision to bind,

Jesus was me and put upon Him, *This Body of Color.*

THIS BODY OF COLOR: FOUR SIMPLE WORDS

The Creator of Earth, in human form, hung in full sacredness on a Configured Tree for *This Body of Color*.

The Repairer for all sacred bodies that would hang from a Seeing Tree is *This Body of Color*.

Covering persecutions due to the intrinsic nature of warm grounded hues redeemed *This Body of Color*.

Surveying more than minds could conceive and eyes fain to see how to till is *This Body of Color*. Planted. Rooted in whose He is; the Plan, the Purpose and the Power of the Black seed is *This Body of Color*.

That's why I stay. Four simple words.

OUR ROAD TRIP TO JESUS

HAYLEY AND MILLIE FLETCHER

Hayley Fletcher is fourteen years old. She enjoys the performing arts and has been involved in several plays. She loves to sing, act, and listen to music and audiobooks. Hayley is a great student and friend; she always finds ways to involve others. She loves anything chocolate.

Millie Fletcher is thirteen years old. She is very athletic and excels in several sports, including basketball and volleyball. Millie is sensitive and outgoing and makes sure everyone around her is included. Millie enjoys animals, especially horses. She loves music, dancing, and making videos. The sisters live in Utah with their parents.

We are Hayley and Millie Fletcher. We are Black, adopted members of The Church of Jesus Christ of Latter-day Saints. We live in an area dominated by White culture. We are both biracial—our birth moms are White, and our birth dads are Black. Being the only brown faces at church and school is not easy. Just being teenage girls is not easy, especially if you are tall, brown, and have huge hair. Most girls our age just want to fit in, but for us that's impossible. We stand out and are forced to stand up. Being different makes us tough; it makes us sensitive; it makes us powerful when we tell our stories.

Some days we get tired. People touch our hair, ask us if we play basketball, and assume that our birth moms were on drugs. We have heard and been called the N-word more times than we can count, and our family has experienced racism in many ways since our arrival. When things get really tough, we talk about Jesus: how He treated others and the type of person that He was. In our eyes, Jesus is more like us than most people realize. His skin was probably brown because He was a Jew from the Middle East. He was adopted because Joseph was not His biological father. He stood out and was different in who

He was and the things that He taught. Jesus was cool! He loved everyone and set the perfect example of how we should love each other and appreciate our differences. Jesus loved to be different.

In October 2020, after months of homeschool, quarantine, and racial tension, our mom put us in the car, and we drove five thousand miles across the country to learn more about our roots, our history, and Jesus. Mom called it our find-our-roots-and-Jesus road trip. We called it our Mom-may-be-having-a-nervous-breakdown road trip. Either way, our focus turned to the road and our Savior. We found Jesus along the way, with family, friends, historical heroes, and strangers. Let's just say that we belted the song "Jesus Take the Wheel" throughout our trip; it was hilarious. It was our theme song. We left with tears and big plans to find some peace. We hoped the voices of the past would teach us about the future. Throughout the trip we read the New Testament. We learned about Jesus's life and mission. We found His love and compassion through others in our studies and as we toured historic Civil Rights movement sites across the country.

Being different makes us tough; it makes us sensitive; it makes us powerful when we tell our stories. . . . When things get really tough, we talk about Jesus.

Our first visit was to Millie's Grandma V in Oklahoma. Our mom took us to Grandma V because she could tell us things and could relate to our issues with racism because she's a Black woman. Our mom loves us, but she also knows that because she is White, she will never understand everything we go through. Grandma V talked to us about being strong, Black women. She talked about her own experiences with racism and her daily struggles to live with bias and ignorance. She not only understood our trials—she was living them. We spent the night in Grandma V's home, and on Sunday morning we found Jesus at the Corinth Baptist Church, which we attended with her. We shouted praise, listened to an amazing pastor, and rocked the world with music and song. After church we stood in her driveway and prayed together. Then we tearfully hugged goodbye and turned our car toward Mississippi.

Our next visit was to the home of Medgar Evers in Jackson, Mississippi. We sat outside his home and talked about his murder and about his wife, Myrlie, and their little children who had found him in his driveway. It was quiet in our car as our mom told us his story. We learned about sacrifice, determination, and purpose.

Jesus taught the people that to follow Him meant denying self and taking up their cross (see Luke 9:23). He said: "For whosoever will save his life shall lose it: but whosoever will lose his life for my sake, the same shall save it" (Luke 9:24). Mr. Medgar did as Jesus asked. He took up the "cross" of Civil Rights, working to improve life for others, like Jesus did. Though Mr. Medgar's reward from Jesus wasn't received in this life, surely in the next Jesus will remember him and bless him for his work. Like Jesus's, Mr. Medgar's mission and life were short, and like Jesus's, his legacy has lived on.

As we drove at night across Mississippi, we learned about Mamie Till and her son Emmett. Emmett was our age when he was murdered by some White men for something he didn't do. As we drove, the roads were dark and rainy, and we traveled over bridges similar to the one young Emmett was tossed off of. Ms. Mamie was so strong. She is one of our mom's heroes. Ms. Mamie sacrificed her own grief and trauma to open her son's casket to let the world see her son and what racial hatred had done to him. Her decision literally changed the course of the Civil Rights movement. Jesus's mom, Mary, must have felt like Ms. Mamie. Jesus didn't deserve to die either, and Mary also stood by Him following His death. This

> *Jesus didn't deserve to die either, and Mary also stood by Him following His death. This made us realize once again that because Jesus died for us, we will all live again. Emmett and Ms. Mamie will as well.*

made us realize once again that because Jesus died for us, we will all live again. Emmett and Ms. Mamie will as well.

Like so many prophets and heroes of the scriptures, we don't always see the results of our actions. Abinadi didn't know that Alma was even listening, and he later changed the lives of so many as a faithful prophet (see Mosiah 11–17). The same was true for Ms. Mamie. Little did she know at the time that another powerful lady, Rosa Parks, saw her strength and was inspired. Three months later, Ms. Rosa took a seat on a bus and contributed to the Civil Rights movement to change our country for the better.

We found Jesus in New Orleans on the steps of the school Ruby Bridges attended. Our feet climbed the same steps, and we took photos in front of her school. Ruby's experience reminded us of Jesus. How many angry crowds did Jesus endure? But He kept His head up and kept walking. We have also endured racism in school, and just like Ruby we also deserve an education.

> We talked a lot about Jesus and learned that He understands us because He endured similar situations.

During our trip, we laughed and we cried and we talked about important things. We talked a lot about Jesus and learned that He understands us because He endured similar situations. We visited historic places of our Black ancestry. We reflected on the shores of New Orleans, where enslaved persons were dragged from ships, chained and helpless. Like them, Jesus had been bound and taken. Like our enslaved Ancestors, He was beaten and mocked. Jesus didn't deserve that horrible treatment, and neither did our Ancestors. He suffered for those who were forced onto the auction blocks of New Orleans; He knew their suffering and struggles (see Mark 15:15–21).

We found ourselves in Montgomery, Alabama, on the steps of the Dexter Avenue King Memorial Baptist Church, Martin Luther King Jr.'s first church. We sat on the church steps and talked about his mission, his family, and how we recognized part of Jesus in the way that Dr. King lived. Like Jesus, Dr. King spent his life preaching to people to follow God, love others, and become united. As we continued our journey, we followed Dr. King to Florida, into Georgia, and lastly to Memphis, Tennessee, to the Lorraine Motel, where he was killed. By the time we reached Memphis, Dr. King was like a friend to us. We had listened to his speeches, stood in front of his homes, and marched where he had marched. We asked ourselves why anyone would kill someone so young, so motivational, and so important to this world. We sat in front of the hotel where he died, and our thoughts turned to our Savior; we asked the same questions. Jesus was also young, powerful, and full of hope. He taught us to love each other and to endure every hardship that comes our way. He suffered equally for everyone no matter their race, religion, or location.

> *All roads are more difficult to travel when alone. In the end, Jesus remains our best travel companion and our great tour guide. He has taught us to follow the map He has made for us. He is the Way, the Truth, and the Life.*

When we finally pulled back into our own driveway, we were different people. We had new knowledge, determination, and hope. We had walked on sacred ground. We had been inspired by countless people and their stories. Most importantly, we had found Jesus and knew Him better than we had before our trip.

We've thought so much about our road trip across the country. We've thought a lot about the road we have been asked to travel as Black girls in America. All roads have twists and turns. All roads have dips and crashes. All roads are more difficult to travel when alone. In the end, Jesus remains our best travel companion and our great tour guide. He has taught us to follow the map He has made for us. He is the Way, the Truth, and the Life (see John 14:6), and that's better than any GPS system we could ever buy.

Sometimes we learn the most on the unlit roads, the lonely stretches of travel, and the journeys that dip into the past but guide us into the future. We pray that people will learn that diversity is good, that racism is an awful sin, that Jesus loves us all because we are part of His beautiful family, and that we are all created in His image with great purpose. We can find Him anywhere in this world if we just take the time to look.

ONE SEEKING TO KNOW AND LEARN

ABNER LEONARD HOWELL

1878–1966

Abner Leonard Howell was born to Paul Cephas Howell and Eliza Sharp, both formerly enslaved, in Mansfield, Louisiana. Abner was a gifted football player who led his high school team to victory in 1900 and aided his college team to win the national collegiate football title in 1902, 1903, and 1904.[1]

You wanted to know about my conversion to the Church. Well, that was just natural for one seeking to know and learn. I was born just 13 years after the slaves were set free, and grew up just when the Black people were having their hardest time to understand what it was to be free. Before I was in my teens I wondered many times why I was a different color to the other boys. Little by little I was told that I was cursed and could not go to heaven when I died, but was doomed to go to hell with the devil and burn forever.

One day, when the boys were telling me these things, I was so touched that I began to cry. While in this frame of mind, [one of the adults] came along and wanted to know what was wrong and why I was crying. So I told him. He comforted me with a

> *A great load was lifted from my heart and mind, and my eyes were opened.*

---

1. See Margaret Young, "Abner Leonard Howell (1877–1966)," July 23, 2013, Black Past, accessed September 1, 2021, https://www.blackpast.org/african-american-history/howell-abner-leonard-1877-1966/.

few kind words and took me to his house, a block away. He got the Book of Mormon and turned to the 26th chapter of 2nd Nephi, and last verse.[2] He then said read this, which I did. When I was through reading, a great load was lifted from my heart and mind, and my eyes were opened, and I read more and more. I thought how great that was! The words "all are alike unto God."

I could not find anything in the Bible that pleased me so much as what I had just read in the Book of Mormon. I never discussed my thoughts with anyone. I just dreamed day after day to myself. I did not tell my mother about this as she did not want to join the Church. The people who owned her in slavery time were Methodist and she always said that was good enough for her. With this background I grew up joining no church but with all Latter-day Saint ideas, ways and thoughts.

I did not go to church much until I was married and my first child was old enough to be baptized. My wife and I were baptized and then was when I became active in the Church and have been ever since.

[The Church] had started the church welfare plan and I began to work for the Church. I helped build all the buildings in the Welfare Center. I did other work for the Church. I tore down the last of the old tithing office.

That was in 1936–1939 when I spent those happy days working for the Church. I spent most of the forties with organized labor being a member of the city federation of labor. Later I was on the Executive Board of the Salt Lake Boy Scouts Council. I also served two years on the Community Chest, and was on the Welfare Board. I served two years on the State Senate door. About this time I wanted to see some of the East and South so I went to [see a member of the Presiding

---

2. 2 Nephi 26:33 reads, "For none of these iniquities come of the Lord; for he doeth that which is good among the children of men; and he doeth nothing save it be plain unto the children of men; and he inviteth them all to come unto him and partake of his goodness; and he denieth none that come unto him, black and white, bond and free, male and female; and he remembereth the heathen; and all are alike unto God, both Jew and Gentile."

Bishopric] and had a talk. He had told me if I ever decided to go, to come in and talk with him. The following is the letter he gave me:

> June 20, 1951. To whom it may concern: This will introduce to you Brother and Sister Abner L. Howell (colored) who are good members of our church, being members of the Evergreen Ward here in Salt Lake City.
>
> Brother and Sister Howell have been faithful throughout the years and are now enjoying what they have looked forward to for a long time; namely a trip through the Southern and Eastern parts of the United States. We have invited them to call upon our people, the missionaries, and Saints wherever convenient.
>
> Any courtesies extended to them will be very much appreciated.

We left as soon as we got the letter for Boston.[3] At the mission there as we arrived were missionaries, and there was a homesick girl, who, after hugging my wife and finding that we were from Utah, she was made a happy, well girl. I was happier than her to think a few words could make such a change in anyone.

Our next stop was Cincinnati, as this was a special stop to see a colored Brother and his family. [One of the Brethren of the Church] gave me the address, as he had baptized two members when he was on his mission and thought a lot of the family.

On arriving in Cincinnati we had a sadder outlook. We found that society had creeped into religion. Most of the members lived across the river on the Kentucky side and some of them did not want the Negro family to come to church. They could only come to church once a month, on fast Sunday. Cincinnati was at that time only a branch. I

---

3. "The couple was asked by Church officials to go to the Southern states to look into the possibility of establishing segregated congregations. They took a letter of introduction signed by a Church Apostle." Young, "Abner Leonard Howell (1877–1966)."

went Sunday with the colored brother. His family had been receiving missionaries for many years. I went in the gospel doctrine class and as I had already had the lesson they were on, I was able to answer many questions. When Sunday School was out I gave my letter to the bishop to read, and after reading he said, "How long will you be here?" and I said, "Two days." He said, "Would you like to say a few words at Sacrament tonight?" I said, "Sure I would." Then it was that he told me of the feeling of some of the members of the Church about the Negro family. He told me to be easy on the "haters." I said, "I will be so nice they will like me." He said they all sat on the right side, the leader had long bushy hair.

When [one of the Church Brethren] heard that I was going down South he called me into his office to talk to me. He said, "I want to tell you something. You have been raised in Utah and you don't know those people. You won't get treated there like you do here. Be *very* careful, what you say, and where you go. They will always be right and you will be wrong, but say nothing, you will then get along."

That afternoon I asked the Lord to lead me in the right way that night. The bishop had said about ten minutes. Somehow that last verse in the 26th chapter of 2nd Nephi said "Read me." I talked a short while on brotherhood. Then I took the Book of Mormon and started to read, but my time was up—I looked at the bishop. He said, "Go on." I finished the entire evening by looking at the bishop several times and each time getting the go ahead sign. As I had expected, those people came to shake my hand and greeted me as a good Latter-day Saint. One man said, "I did not know there were such things in the Book of Mormon." That Negro family was permitted to come and were made welcome by all the members of the church.

I went to Atlanta next and had a wonderful time. There were 15 missionaries there, and they all read the letter I had [with me]. I did not have time to stay long in Atlanta, as I wanted to get to Shreveport where the new mission was being set up. We stayed overnight there. There were no missionaries there.

We had an experience that is worth mentioning. I was on the train between Jackson and Meridian, Mississippi, when a lady and her grown daughter got on the train. She began to look at me and my wife. I don't know what she thought, but she finally said, "Are you a preacher?" I said, "No lady—I am a Mormon." She said, "What is a Mormon?" I told her about the Prophet Joseph. When she got off the train in Meridian, I gave her the only tract I had. It was *Baptism: The Birth of Water and the Spirit* by Orson F. Whitney. I did not get her name, but two years later on the temple grounds she tapped me on the back and said, "I know you." She told me about the time on the train, then said, "I'm here for my first conference."

My wife Martha died in May 1954, and as I wanted to go to California I went to visit my sister who had been living there some 35 years. I placed my recommend in the Arlington Ward from where I acted as guide at the dedication of the Los Angeles Temple.[4]

I spoke to many firesides and seminaries and [at university]. [One institute president] said I could please his classes better than he could sometimes, as they liked to see me come. I talked to a class . . . in Long Beach, that had no standing room, all wanting to know why I was a Mormon.[5]

---

4. "Although the Church restricted its priesthood from anyone of African lineage, Howell was given a card in 1965 naming him an 'Honorary High Priest.'" Young, "Abner Leonard Howell (1877–1966)."
5. This essay is from a personal letter to Kate B. Carter from Abner L. Howell (A. L. Howell), transcribed in *The Story of the Negro Pioneer*, 57–60; used by permission of Daughters of Utah Pioneers; includes some updates to spelling and grammar; all names mentioned in original letter have been removed for privacy.

STAUNCH MEMBERS OF THIS RELIGION

MARY LUCILLE PERKINS BANKHEAD

1902–1994

Mary Lucille Perkins Bankhead is a descendant of Black American Latter-day Saint pioneer Green Flake and is related through marriage to another Black American Latter-day Saint pioneer, Jane Elizabeth Manning James. She became the first Relief Society president of the Genesis Group when it was formed October 19, 1971.[1] Lucille was a member of the Alva Keller Camp of the Daughters of Utah Pioneers, where she served as its secretary and treasurer.[2]

When the new religion was born, brought about by Divine power, its members suffered mob violence, lynching,[3] pillaging, and then this stalwart band of converts sought a home in the west.

In this group were some Black brothers and sisters. They too worked, pushed handcarts, their children drove the cattle, yes, some died on the trail, yet most of those who survived remained staunch members of this religion. They knew that every man had to help

---

1. See Tarienne Mitchell, "Lucille Bankhead: Defender of African American Rights," Better Days 2020, accessed September 1, 2021, https://www.utahwomenshistory.org/bios/lucille-bankhead/.
2. See Kate B. Carter, comp., *The Story of the Negro Pioneer* (Salt Lake City: Daughters of Utah Pioneers, 1965), 30; The Society of Daughters of Utah Pioneers Application for Membership, June 6, 1955; copy given to Alice Faulkner Burch by DUP librarian Pam Carson, July 29, 2021.
3. "Lynching: a form of violence in which a mob, under the pretext of administering justice without trial, executes a presumed offender, often after inflicting torture and corporal mutilation. . . . Statistics of reported lynching in the United States indicate that, between 1882 and 1951, 4,730 persons were lynched, of whom 1,293 were white and 3,437 were black." Geoffrey Abbott, "Lynching," Encyclopedia Britannica, accessed November 22, 2021, https://www.brittanica.com/topic/lynching.

himself with the talents God had given him. They learned to work, and their children were not forgotten, for they were given farms and land chosen by Brigham Young, and through his kindness Negro families were able to stay together.

We who are members of this great Church and came of this pioneer heritage have much to live up to. We must continue to believe in God, to live clean lives and have faith in ourselves and others. Our Heavenly Father in His loving way of doing good, will bless us if we believe in and keep His commandments.[4]

> *We who are members of this great Church and came of this pioneer heritage have much to live up to.*

There is one verse in the Bible that the Lord is no respecter of persons and I've always believed that.[5]

---

4. See Carter, comp., *Story of the Negro Pioneer*, 30.
5. See Mitchell, "Lucille Bankhead: Defender of African American Rights"; and Romans 2:11: "For there is no respect of persons with God."

THIS BODY OF BEING

This Body of Being was designed
by The Great Creators
to stand straight in glory
to sway in music
to dance in praise
to flow in sync with nature.

But you, Colonizer,
want THIS Body of Being to change
to contort to be obscene
to shrink to be less-than
to twist to be inglorious
to melt to be disconnected.

The God and The Ancestors –
The Great Creators of the Being I fill Here –
knew my divine potential
before The Grands were a twinkle.
My Connection to them all
and to Creation
was set before Time measured
into THIS Body of Being.

Eyes without Light cannot See
the Lines
or Beauty
or Spirit
or Depth
or Wisdom
or Eternity
of This Body of Being.

—*Alice Faulkner Burch*

"I, TOO, AM PART OF GOD'S PLAN"

TAYLER JOLLEY

Tayler Jolley is sixteen years old. Adopted at birth, she is growing up in Utah. She lives in a family of ten: two parents and eight kids. She is biologically related to two of her siblings. Tayler is a junior in high school, and she enjoys reading poetry, reading about astronomy, doing photography, and hanging with her friends.

My testimony of Jesus Christ and my journey through the gospel have affected my life in many ways. In my short amount of time on this earth, I have experienced blessings and trials. I have always believed everything happens for a reason, whether that be good or bad, hard or easy—that reason is God's plan. I believe in God's plan so much because I was put on this earth for a reason. As much control as I think I have over my life, God knows every thought and every feeling and every choice I'm going to make or have already made before I even know it myself, because He knows me that well.

> *I have always believed everything happens for a reason, whether that be good or bad, hard or easy— that reason being God's plan.*

I have felt myself pulling away from the Church on multiple occasions. No amount of reading the scriptures in Sunday School or on my own or going to Young Women helped during those times. Nothing helped me feel closer to God. I just gave up and felt like I was a lost cause. Everything that I was so used to doing as a member of the Church started to feel forced and unnatural. I stopped praying, stopped hanging around my family, and stopped being with my good friends who influenced me in good ways. I pushed God and all light out of my life. I felt utterly alone. That was truly a low point in my life, and I hope to never ever feel that way again. Now that I have a better understanding of God's plan and a stronger testimony, I know that I won't have to be in that dark place again.

In the moment of my lowest point I remember silently praying for *anyone* to hear me. In that moment *someone* did hear me. Even though I had given up on God and everything and everyone I believed in, God never wavered on me for a second. The experience was so surreal. Even though God wasn't verbally speaking to me, I felt His voice and words through my entire body, soul, and mind. I felt His love for me. I felt His hand on my back, not pushing me or serving as a crutch to hold on to, but as a place of balance from which I could push myself forward—like in swimming when you hold to the edge of the pool, both feet on the wall, and push off to go forward into a backstroke.

Since that day I have not questioned God's love for me or whether I have someone when I feel like no one is there for me or hears me. I have decided to continue my spiritual growth and to continue my journey in the gospel. I have decided to continue the journey that is my life.

In my sixteen years of life, I have come across a lot of racism because I'm African American and because I'm different from the majority of the population where I was raised and live. The looks, glances, and downright stares that come my way because of the color of my skin don't go unnoticed by me. I have been treated differently but thought for a while that it hadn't affected me. I later learned that it had and that I had soaked in how I was being treated and let it affect my faith in God and who I believed I was to Him and in His plan. Like soaking in the bathtub until the water gets cold, I had become cold from soaking in the non-truths and meanness from others, and I was becoming colder the longer I stayed in it.

Recently I watched a really good movie with my mom and sister. The main character, an African American woman, said something that made me think. I took what she said to heart because I can relate to it on an everyday basis. What that character said reminded me that the same God made us all. He made me and all African Americans. He made all White people too—both the ones who are nice to me and the ones who are mean to me. The only difference between me and a White person is the color of our skin. In the Book of Mormon, Moroni speaks in anger to his enemy Ammoron. Ammoron, who doesn't believe in God, tells Moroni something that maybe he had forgotten: "If it so be that there is [a God], we know not but that he hath made us as well as you" (Alma 54:21). I walk and talk the same as White people do. I sleep and eat the same as White people do. Even if they think of me as their enemy, the truth is still the truth: the same God made us all.

Heavenly Father has blessed me with my amazing friends and family. My family isn't like many others, since my siblings and I don't look like our parents. My parents are White, and my brothers and sisters and I are all African American. Not looking like my parents and our skin not being the same color does not change the fact that they are my parents, given to me by God. I get the same blessings from honoring my parents as those children who do look like their parents. "*Honour thy father* and thy *mother*: that thy days may be long upon the land which the Lord thy God giveth thee," we are promised (Exodus 20:12). If I keep that commandment, the accompanying blessing is mine too. Blood and skin color aren't the only things that define us as family.

> *God made us all. He made me and all African Americans. He made all White people too—both the ones who are nice to me and the ones who are mean to me.*

"I, TOO, AM PART OF GOD'S PLAN"

Since the same God made us all and we all call Him "Father," then we are all brothers and sisters. *We—all of us—are family.*

Just like my skin color doesn't make me any less human than a White person, it also doesn't make me any less a child of God. "So we, being many, are one body in Christ, and every one members one of another" (Romans 12:5). From the scriptures I have learned that I am a daughter of God and that I, too, am part of God's plan. I'm blessed to learn that while still young.

> *Blood and skin color aren't the only things that define us as family. Since the same God made us all and we all call Him "Father," then we are all brothers and sisters.* We—all of us—are family.

THE PATH WE TAKE—
DO I BELONG?

GLORIA TALLEY WILKINSON

Gloria Wilkinson is married with four children and soon to be fourteen grandchildren. She worked with the International Affairs Office in Washington, DC, from 1992 to 1997. For almost twenty years, she and her family lived in Salt Lake City, Utah, where she was active in community and political affairs. Gloria retired in 2015, and she and her husband now reside in Maryland.

Oftentimes I review my life, as many do. I am reminded of my third son's poem entitled "The Path Not Taken," which is about making choices and his decision to follow the Book of Mormon. His poem reminds me of Robert Frost's poem "The Road Not Taken." Both poems concern the choices we make, as well as the challenges we face as we journey through life. No one gets through this life without having challenges—some hard, some very painful, some life-altering. And then some become joys. Some can be all four, just at different times.

I was raised in two small, African American communities. Both consisted of extended family and close acquaintances. Although my school was integrated, the schools were not close to my community. Therefore, my classmates and I did not have the opportunity to socialize outside of school.

The churches I attended were small, located in segregated, rural communities. The members were all Black. The Reverend Dr. Martin Luther King Jr. once said that "11 o'clock on Sunday morning is the most segregated hour of Christian America."[1] For me, that was correct. I belonged to the youth choir, and we sang soulful hymns and heard the shouts of "Hallelujah!" and "Amen!" from the congregation. I knew the people and enjoyed being around and learning from them.

When Winston and I married, we moved away from our childhood homes and began our journey to create our own traditions and find our own path. We attended several churches, looking for one that satisfied our desire to belong and that would provide us with the answers we were seeking, as well as the acceptance that was given to us in our youth. It took us several years to find the right niche.

In 1981, Winston met Elder V. Dallas Merrell[2] at a political function and was prompted to ask him about his religion. We were invited to his home, where he had also invited the missionaries to share the gospel with us. The information they shared was interesting, although somewhat different than what I had learned in my church. However, many of my questions about life after death and eternity were answered.

The more I listened, the more apprehensive I became. The lesson was taking a different path than I expected. Most importantly, it was taking me from my upbringing and my heritage. But for some reason, I also felt this was the right path. We took the lessons for several months, and in September 1981 our family joined The Church of Jesus Christ of Latter-day Saints.

Less than fifteen years earlier, the country had been embattled in a civil rights struggle. That struggle was still going on, although more subtly. Commingling between the races on a social scale remained very limited, and even more so when it came to worship. The Church too

---

1. Martin Luther King Jr., "Meet the Press," April 17, 1960.
2. V. Dallas Merrell served in The Church of Jesus Christ of Latter-day Saints as president of the Utah Salt Lake City South Mission, 1986–1989, regional representative, 1989–1992; and General Authority Seventy, 1992–1997. He passed on February 21, 2019, survived by his long-time sweetheart, Karen Dixon Merrell. Mention of Elder Merrell is by permission of his wife, Sister Merrell.

still had its issues. The ban on Black people having the priesthood had been reversed only a short time earlier, in June 1978, some 148 years after the Church had been established. Some individual Church members still struggled interacting with Black Latter-day Saints and with Black men holding the priesthood.

On the day of our baptism, we were late for the sacrament service. At the time we had three children, ages ten, six, and four. During the previous weeks before our baptism, we had been told there were Black members in that ward. Imagine my surprise when we entered the chapel the day of our baptism and saw the church was packed, but not one—no, not one—was Black. Now, remember this was the first time I had worshipped with White people. There was a sea of White faces. Every seat in the room was taken except those saved by our friends the Merrells. I panicked. Was I ready for this change?

After the sacrament meeting ended, I was ready to go home and leave my husband at the church. This whole experience was a bit much for me. Dallas sensed my hesitation and asked me to walk with him. For forty-five minutes we walked around the parking lot of the church and talked about Church doctrine and what it would mean for me and my family. Round and round that parking lot we walked. My questions and concerns were about my children, my family, my traditions, and my heritage. What was to become of those? Winston and my oldest son were ready. I was still hesitant.

> *My questions and concerns were about my children, my family, my traditions, and my heritage. What was to become of those?*

I was baptized that day not because I had a testimony, but because of the faith exercised by my husband and son. Had I known the history of the Church, I most likely would not have joined. It was only after I was baptized that I began to read in depth about the Church. I learned about the priesthood ban for Black men and women. I learned from other Black members about their experiences with the Church and about the Church's relationship to the Black community. And I saw the negative reactions of White members to my family and me. Maybe learning all this about the Church *after* I was baptized was part of the Lord's design for me.

We have been members of the Church for forty years. There has been joy. There have also been disappointments and challenges.

When I read historical books, especially those about African American history, I review the index first to determine if my family names are mentioned. I want to know if my family is represented in the context of that particular book and if they played a part in that specific situation. I also review the index first because for so long African Americans have been written out of history, and our contributions to society have been ignored or misrepresented.

As a public relations professional, I know that if individuals cannot identify with the product or do not see themselves represented in a company's marketing materials, those individuals have to decide if the company truly wants them as customers or clients. President M. Russell Ballard mentioned in his April 2021 general conference talk a study produced by the Mayo Clinic. The study, he said, stated: "We cannot separate the importance of a sense of belonging from our mental and physical health," and, President Ballard added, "our spiritual health." He continued: "Having a sense of belonging is so important. Nearly every aspect of our lives is organized around some form of belonging to something."[3]

Because of the history of the Church, I look for African Americans in Church literature and marketing materials. This is a worldwide church, and it disturbs me that leadership, pictures, and so on do not reflect its membership. I also began to search Church magazines and literature to see if African Americans were included. I went so far as to

---

3. M. Russell Ballard, "Hope in Christ," *Liahona*, May 2021.

look at past conference editions and count the number of pictures of Black people captured in the magazine. When I first began the review, there were few pictures of African Americans. In the last few years, however, representation of African Americans has increased.

When we lived in Sandy, Utah, I served in the Primary presidency in my ward. The ward had people of several ethnicities, so the presidency wanted to ensure the children saw themselves in the pictures that hung on the walls. Seeing people who look like them is so important for children, for us all; it develops good mental health, it builds positive self-esteem, and it creates feelings of connectivity and belonging.

Since my baptism, my questions have changed: Who is the Church for? Do I belong? Am I wanted in the Church? If The Church of Jesus Christ of Latter-day Saints is for all people, including Black people, then we should all be represented.

As young parents, my husband and I wanted to ensure our children had a strong sense of who they were growing up—of their divine nature. We wanted them to know they were children of the Most High God, made in His image. We taught them to be proud of who they were, to know their heritage, and to respect others.

We sang a song when I was growing up called "Jesus Loves the Little Children."[4]

> *Jesus loves the little children*
> *All the children of the world*
> *Brown and Black and White*
> *They are precious in His sight.*
> *Jesus loves the little children of the world.*

That song taught me that God made me and made all of us in

---

4. "Jesus Loves the Little Children," late 1800s; lyrics by Reverend Clarence Herbert Woolston (1856–1927); third line has been slightly modified; in the public domain.

different shapes, in different colors, and with different abilities. He loves me. He loves us all. Each time I sang that song, it was an affirmation that God truly loved me.

It is important that I, my children, and my grandchildren see people who look like us in those leading the Church. It is important that we see people who look like us on the pages of magazines and books and in pictures that are published by the Church. That has been my calling: as an African American, I want White people to understand that people of color need to see ourselves in order to feel welcomed and to feel a sense of belonging.

Seeing people who look like them is so important for children, for us all; it develops good mental health, it builds positive self-esteem, and it creates feelings of connectivity and belonging.

Two of our four children are no longer practicing members of the Church. Unfortunately, they did not feel they were welcomed. Winston and I have been members of the Church for forty years. We have continued to serve in various callings and have met many wonderful people. We have experienced joys. Even though challenges continue, I have stayed because my deepest questions have been answered. I exercise my faith by looking past the people and concentrating on our Heavenly Father. I have faith in our Heavenly Father and know that He loves me.

Did I take the right path? I think so. "I took the one less traveled by, and that has made all the difference."[5]

---

5. Robert Frost, "The Road Not Taken."

IN THE SAME MANNER

EUGENE ORR

Eugene Orr is the son of David Orr and Martha Wilder Orr. He has four children. He is a founding member of the Genesis Group and was the second counselor in the first Genesis Group presidency. At seventy-six years old, Eugene has been a member of the Church for fifty-four years. Eugene lives in Canada, where he works as a naturopathic health counselor.

The year 1946 in the United States of America was at the advent of the Civil Rights movement. For Black people the events of this movement created some favorable circumstances, such as greater freedom to worship God, and some unfavorable circumstances, such as the continued denial of some freedom of speech and voting rights. It seemed that Black people and freedom were a contradiction.

Being Black in the United States has always been a struggle; joys and triumphs were shadowed by feelings of sadness, hopelessness, emptiness, and despair. In the aftermath of slavery and amid Jim Crow laws, many Southern Black people struggled to find equality and justice in a system never designed for us to excel.

> *Being Black in the United States has always been a struggle; joys and triumphs were shadowed by feelings of sadness, hopelessness, emptiness, and despair.*

While we had some freedoms and liberties, Black people often found it hard to access and benefit from those freedoms and liberties—like going to school. We could go, but it wasn't always possible. I was so excited to go to school. I was curious and loved to learn, so naturally I thought of myself as a stellar student. After finishing grade one, I was looking forward to grade two.

But the following school year, we were pulled from school to help work in the cotton field alongside our parents. Although disappointed, we never grumbled or complained. It was a year of witnessing how hard my parents worked to provide and care for us kids. I learned that nothing came easy or without dedication and sacrifice.

I was born a Southern Baptist! Being Baptist taught me many things about God and Jesus Christ, but still I felt there was something more. My inner thoughts were always beckoning, summoning me to seek more understanding. I did not know then that feeling was Heavenly Father guiding and directing me in the direction that was best for me. While recuperating from rheumatic fever and missing yet another year of school, when I was strong enough, I would go into the yard and lie down on the green grass on hot summer days and look up into the big blue sky, searching to see my Heavenly Father and wondering if He was looking back at me.

> *My inner thoughts were always beckoning, summoning me to seek more understanding. I did not know then that feeling was Heavenly Father guiding and directing me in the direction that was best for me.*

After Sunday services, I would go out to the big chinaberry tree and line up soda pop bottles to resemble a congregation. The lady bottles had hair made of cornsilk that I placed carefully so it spilled from the bottlenecks. Then I would position a plain ole pop bottle next to each lady to represent the men. And I would preach, sharing the message of God. I would drag my handkerchief across my brow to soak up the sweat and then my lips to catch the spittle, just like my preacher. That congregation of pop bottles would get the best sermons of their lives! Sometimes, people would witness me saving those pop-bottle souls and say, "That boy will grow up to be a preacher one day."

In 1955, when I was about nine years old, I had a poignant spiritual experience. I dreamed of a heavenly messenger, clothed in white robes; the sky surrounded him like the misty pink clouds of a beautiful sunset. We sat on the bench against the wall of the local grocery store. He put his arm around me as we talked. I felt comforted. What he told me I cannot remember to this day, but I knew it was good. After that night, my whole life changed for the better.

We lived on a big farm with cotton fields, sweet potato, watermelon, and peanut crops. We had animals too, and my dad would butcher and smoke meat in his smokehouse every October. One day my father told the family that we were moving to Orlando, Florida, because he wanted better education opportunities for us children. My dad soon had a buyer for the farm and agreed to sell it for $3,500. The seller presented a document and told my dad that he was giving him $350 as a down payment. Not being able to read, my dad listened intently and signed the document, not knowing that he had just sold the farm for $350, not $3,500, as he believed.

Now we didn't have enough money to move, and we had no place to stay. My parents moved us to Ashburn, Virginia, into the projects because that was all we could afford. Dad decided to go to Orlando and prepare a place. Dad sent money to us, and my parents scrimped and saved every penny. After almost two years, Dad had saved enough money to rent a small house and take us all to Orlando.

At age eighteen, I thought I was a man and worked hard to prove it to my dad. I wanted his respect and for him to treat me like a man. I had plans to go on to university and become a math teacher. After my girlfriend became pregnant we decided to marry. We learned accountability and responsibility. We were both too young to be parents. At age nineteen, we both left school, got married, and welcomed a son into this world. We had our second son when we were twenty. At twenty-two years old, we divorced.

I didn't realize it at the time, but looking back, I know the Lord was preparing me to hear and partake of the restored gospel of Jesus Christ. I worked with the Job Corps program for a while, and it took me from Florida to California. Then around my birthday in 1968, the Job Corps transferred me to work in Clearfield, Utah, a town just outside of Salt Lake City. I mentioned the transfer to Utah to a friend of mine. He told me, "Those Mormons think they have the only true gospel here on earth, and they do *not* like Black people." My first thought was that at least one of those statements had to be wrong. His statement was my introduction to the Latter-day Saints.

At my new job, my coworkers and I worked Monday through Friday, and Friday evenings we'd jump on the bus and go to Salt Lake City for the weekends. It was a time to blow off steam, socialize, and see the big city. One rainy night as I was walking into the bus station, a beautiful blonde woman with a newspaper over her head ran out of the swinging glass door and right into me. Meeting Lei was like a movie, where boy meets girl quite by accident. But I believe it was intended.

> *He told me, "Those Mormons think they have the only true gospel here on earth, and they do* not *like Black people." My first thought was that at least one of those statements had to be wrong.*

When we bumped into each other, the newspaper she held to protect herself from the rain fell to the ground. I bent down to pick it up and offered my arm and my umbrella, which she graciously accepted, and I walked her to her car parked just a few steps away. I felt the urge to ask her if she knew any Latter-day Saints.

Lei looked at me and said, "Yeah, I am one!"

Feeling encouraged and comfortable, I asked, "So you guys believe you have the true religion?"

Again, she replied, "Yes."

I asked, "And you don't like Black people?"

She retorted, "Who said we don't like Black people?"

I replied that that was what I was told. The rain fell around us, and she invited me to get into her car so she could tell me more about The Church of Jesus Christ of Latter-day Saints and the Church's view of Black people. Now, let's remember what was happening during this period: Black people were questioning whether Dr. King's 1963 dream would bring about the racial equity and community we needed, and many White people were reserved about the dream, and some even opposed it. Racial tensions in the US were high. So for her to invite me into her car without reservation spoke to her heart and her faith. She must have been prompted and felt protected by the Spirit, having faith that all was well.

I accepted her invitation and got into her car. I intently listened as she attempted to explain the curse upon Black people. She told me that I was cursed and of the seed of Cain and the whole works. She didn't do too good of a job! But still I wasn't put off. She must have sensed it too, because she then invited me to meet with the missionaries at her home the following weekend to learn more. Feeling excited, I agreed. We exchanged numbers, and I left for Clearfield.

Over the week, she called to confirm that the missionaries would meet with me on the weekend. I was looking forward to asking my questions and getting some answers. In my first meeting, we ended up having the first and second missionary lessons. While some of the sisters' comments did not appeal to me, especially what they said about Black people, I remained curious and scheduled my third discussion with Lei and the missionaries for the following weekend.

One of the sister missionaries told me that if I were baptized into the Church *and* become righteous *enough*, my skin would change from black to white, just like hers, and I wouldn't be Black anymore. I didn't know the Holy Ghost as I do today, but a voice whispered the truth to me, even then. I knew in my heart and mind that all she said about Black people wasn't true, so I didn't dwell on that part. I am grateful for the still, small voice I heard that day. The Holy Ghost comforted and assured me about what was and what wasn't truth. I recognized that there was always a fourth being present in our discussions, and He was full of truth and knowledge.

During this time, Lei started taking me to church with her. The first time I went, she also invited the man who rented the upstairs apartment where she lived. His name was David, and he was Jewish. David was also looking into the Church. There we were on Sunday morning in an all-White congregation—a single White woman with a Black man and a Jewish man. Many heads turned and probably speculated about this odd trio. Nonetheless, we continued to go, and David and I became great friends. I often think how brave and unapologetic Lei was. She followed wherever God moved her no matter what others said around her.

I continued the missionary lessons, and I soon found myself ready to commit to baptism. Much of what I learned during the discussions resonated as true, but I still had no understanding of the Church's racial restrictions. Again, Lei stepped in and introduced me to a Black member of the Church, Darius Gray. I had learned that Lei was something of an amazing cook, and over dinner with Darius, we discussed Black people and the priesthood. After our visit, I asked myself if I believed in the gospel of Jesus Christ. Was it true? It was then I decided to fast and pray as the missionaries had suggested. It was a good thing Lei had just nourished me because I was determined to find my answers. I prayed and fasted, and on the third day the still, small voice spoke to me, and I knew without doubt that the Book of Mormon and the Church were true. I have come to know that voice as the Holy Ghost; He had testified to me then and many times. The Spirit Himself bore witness, and I could not deny, hide, or forget.

That was how I received my testimony.

Lei, the missionaries, and Darius all were instruments of our Heavenly Father, and through them the Holy Spirit pressed upon my soul His truth. After all these years, through every trial, every tribulation, every joy, and every blessing, I have remained firm and solid in my belief. I determined that I would never sway from God and His truth for as long as I lived.

On Saturday, August 24, 1968, I was baptized at the tabernacle in Salt Lake City. I sat in this huge room and waited for my name to be called. My mind swirled with thoughts of having a smoke. While I had quit smoking long enough to be baptized, at this moment I wanted one bad. I nervously waited, then I finally heard my name, "Eugene Orr." I got up, walked to the baptismal font, and stepped down into the water. The brother took my hand, spoke a prayer, and laid me in the water, covering my face. As he pulled me up from the water, I had no more thoughts or desire for my bad habits.

> *I knew in my heart and mind that all she said about Black people wasn't true, so I didn't dwell on that part. I am grateful for the still, small voice I heard that day. The Holy Ghost comforted and assured me about what was and what wasn't truth. I recognized that there was always a fourth being present in our discussions, and He was full of truth and knowledge.*

A little while later, during a staff meeting at work, people were smoking. I realized at that moment that I hadn't smoked since my baptism, and the smell of it didn't bother me at all then or ever again. I took this as another confirmation that I was on the right path.

Lei and I had started dating that summer before I was baptized, and before summer had ended, I had asked her to marry me. In September, I made a trip back down to Orlando to let my family know of my engagement to Lei. I invited them to Utah in November to join us on our wedding day. I also visited my two boys, and I told my boys' mom that I was remarrying. My news to my family was well received.

Sadly, Lei's family didn't take the news as well as mine did, which was awfully hard on her. But she never wavered. Her mom and a few other cousins attended the wedding, but they held no joy for her. They sat away from everyone else, almost as though they were in mourning. Maybe they were. They believed that by marrying a Black person, she was giving up her divine birthrights and would experience spiritual death. My mom and two of my sisters were able to come up for our wedding, and they took part in and celebrated our union. For Lei and me, our wedding day was the happiest day of our lives.

Eventually I found myself missing my sons and wanting to know them and for them to know Lei and me. I wanted to bring them to Utah to live with us for a while, but I was sure their mom would not be open to that. So we prayed and fasted off and on for weeks to get the answers from our Heavenly Father. Our prayers were answered when my ex-wife agreed the boys could come for six months. When the time came for the boys to go back to their mom, she had decided that the boys would be better off with Lei and me, so six months turned into forever.

This was the beginning of our journey. God guided us over the forty-five years Lei and I shared. He gave us two more children, the priesthood, and temple sealings. Finding the gospel and deepening my faith in Jesus Christ have filled my life with gifts and blessings.

As we began to learn of other Black members of the Church, I found myself eager to make a connection with them. Soon, my wife had reached out to six other members and invited them to our home for what we called the "Black Mormon Reunion" in 1969. The following year, 1970, we organized another gathering, and Sister Lucille, also a Black member, opened her home to forty-eight Black brothers and sisters. At our third gathering in early 1971, we met at Rose Park in Salt Lake City, with thirty-eight Black Church members in attendance.

At this gathering, I met Brother Ruffin Bridgeforth, who had been a member of the Church for about eighteen years, and the Acting President of the Quorum of the Twelve Apostles, Spencer W. Kimball. The Black Latter-day Saints decided to start meeting weekly, and each member agreed on taking turns hosting the group in their home. These meetings were meaningful opportunities for Black Saints to fellowship with one another, learn, and grow in the Church. We were building a community that supported the Black Latter-day Saint experience, which was so needed. Though we believed in the gospel, we did not feel a sense of belonging. Many of us were in interracial relationships, which had negative implications for some Church members. Black people were often treated as invisible and avoided. Although the Church encouraged racial integration, America and the Church still had a long way to go to reach true integration and inclusion.

My family was growing. My wife sincerely wanted a little girl, so we began the adoption process in 1969. While we waited for our little girl to arrive, we learned of a child in my extended family that needed a home. My wife's eyes lit up with joy! She pleaded with me for us to take the child. It was only a matter of days before I found myself saying yes. And so, in the latter part of 1970, we took this child into our home. Although we did not have the daughter we had wanted, we felt blessed to have another son.

He was small and sickly, but my wife moved heaven and earth to heal and strengthen this precious life. She would often invite our home teachers, White men, to our home to anoint and lay their hands on my Black child's head in prayer for his health and strength. It stood out to me that I could not give my child a blessing in the same manner because I, as a Black man, could not hold the priesthood. In late October, we officially adopted our son. Three months later, we learned that our baby girl was here and ready to come home; we had our daughter, and our family was complete.

In May 1971, I reconnected with Darius Gray and Brother Ruffin. I invited them to meet with me in fasting and prayer to ponder why Black men in America were denied the priesthood within the Church. I was eager to ask this and other questions to the leadership of the Church. We fasted and prayed, and soon we had an answer to our prayers—we were to approach the prophet with our concerns.

Being a skillful writer, Brother Darius drafted a letter to our prophet, who was President Joseph Fielding Smith at the time. Then we reached out and secured an appointment with his secretary for May 10. Brother Darius and Brother Ruffin elected me to be the spokesperson at our meeting, which I embraced. I think they saw in me a fire and desire to disrupt and fight for better. So I shared with the prophet's secretary our questions and concerns. At the end of the meeting, he promised to relay our message to President Smith and arrange a meeting with him.

> *We fasted and prayed, and soon we had an answer to our prayers—we were to approach the prophet with our concerns.*

Weeks passed and there was no follow-up. I was growing impatient, so I decided to go to his office again. This time I did not leave until I had a confirmed meeting day and time.

It was not easy attending the meeting. Security was not informed or expecting three Black men demanding to speak with the prophet. Saying we had an appointment alarmed them, and a flurry of activity ensued. We prevailed, and on June 8, 1971, at 8:00 a.m., Brother Ruffin, Darius, and I sat down with three Apostles: Elder Gordon B. Hinckley, Elder Boyd K. Packer, and Elder Thomas S. Monson. This meeting felt monumental to me. The questions we asked were (1) "Why do some Black men in other places in the world have the priesthood and not others?" (2) "When will the Black men in America receive the priesthood?" and (3) "What and how do we teach our children about the differential treatment of Black people in the Church?" Of course, no final resolution or answers came from this meeting, but the six of us decided to continue the conversation and agreed to meet every two weeks.

When we came together, Elder Hinckley sat behind his large desk, with me directly across from him. On Elder Hinckley's right sat Elder Packer and Elder Monson, with Brother Ruffin and Brother Darius directly sitting across from them. We all intuitively took these positions, which aided a round-table discussion of ideas, mutual respect, curiosity, and critical thought, guided by the Spirit.

Not every meeting ended well. It got heated. Sometimes we simply had to walk away. Sometimes we would roar and sometimes cry. Together, we bent our knees in prayer, beseeching our Father in Heaven for guidance and patience. Other times we prayed in solitude, seeking strength and love. We learned to love and respect each other over time, and we agreed on a way forward.

On October 19, 1971, we held an assembly in Salt Lake City with the three Apostles. There were 175 people in attendance. It would have been magnificent if the congregation that day had brought together all the scattered Black members of the Church. Still, it was a beautiful and extraordinary meeting. The Black Mormon Committee decided on the name "Genesis Group," which the Church leaders approved. The name was utterly profound and relevant as we believed that this meeting was truly the beginning of the Black member movement within the Church. After the meeting, Elder Hinckley set apart Brother Ruffin as the president of the Genesis Group. Elder Monson set apart Brother Darius as first counselor, and Elder Packer set me apart as the second counselor. We all conducted ourselves as though we held the priesthood, although we did not. The Genesis Group was permitted to gather in the evening of the first Sunday of each month.

All the auxiliary callings were set apart by a stake president and a high council representative. Sister Lucille became our first Relief Society president. My wife, Lei, accepted the calling as her first counselor, Sister Mildred as her second counselor, and Sister Helena became secretary for both the Relief Society and Primary presidencies.

For all of us Black members, this formation of our own group and having our own Black presidency presiding over it was a giant leap toward racial equity in the Church and beyond. Having representation in our leadership was meaningful—even if it was at a microlevel.

It renewed our hopes and dreams and reinforced our belief in the Church. Since Black men received the priesthood in 1978, Genesis has continued to meet on the first Sunday of the month, though it is no longer recognized as a branch in the Church.

In 1973, I finally had the honor of sitting with the prophet. Of course, the Church had mourned the passing of two prophets by then. We learned the prophet, President Spencer W. Kimball, would be visiting the ward of a dear friend of ours, so we put on our Sunday best and we walked into that ward. We found a pew near the front that would accommodate our family. Sadly, the White members on the pews in front and behind us got up and moved. It was a good thing we weren't there for fellowship, or we would have been hurt and distressed by the actions of these sisters and brothers. We had come to see and hear the message of our prophet.

> *This formation of our own group and having our own Black presidency presiding over it was a giant leap toward racial equity in the Church and beyond. Having representation in our leadership was meaningful. . . . It renewed our hopes and dreams and reinforced our belief in the Church.*

As the meeting ended, President Kimball made his way over to our family and sat down with us. I like to think he remembered me from years back when he had joined us at our gathering at Rose Park. As he spoke with us, he gently held my daughter on his lap while inquiring about the well-being of my family. I will never forget this moment—how at ease and peace I felt. I will never forget how the rest of the congregation watched on—perhaps confused or ashamed. I had met the prophet, and he had held my child! From then on, President Kimball made a point of visiting my home during the holiday season to deliver a fruit basket. It was through President Kimball that the Lord bestowed the priesthood to the Black men of the Church.

My life as a Black man in the Church has been blessed. I am

grateful for all the gifts our Savior has bestowed upon me and my family, for His help during those times of adversity and temptation, and even for complex tests and others ridiculing my faith. I have stumbled, and I have fallen, but always, no matter how dark it seemed, I knelt in prayer to my Heavenly Father. He has continually poured out His love for me, my wife, and my children. He has continually guided me.

> *I will never forget this moment—how at ease and peace I felt. I will never forget how the rest of the congregation watched on—perhaps confused or ashamed. I had met the prophet, and he had held my child!*

"GREEN TREES ARE BENDING"

FOLLOWING WHERE THE HOLY SPIRIT LEADS

"I had another vision or dream that the Elders' work had been recognized in Heaven and my sins had been forgotten and my name was written in Heaven."

—*Len Ross Hope*
1895–1952; baptized 1919

SLAIN IN THE SPIRIT

RODRIC ANTHONY JOHNSON

Rodric Anthony Johnson served a full-time mission in Cape Town, South Africa, December 1998–December 2000. He and his wife were sealed in 2001 in the Atlanta Georgia Temple. They currently reside in Arizona with their seven children. Rodric is a prolific writer, who writes of his spiritual experiences and what he learns from reading the scriptures.

God is a constant in my life, introduced to me through my maternal auntie, Mother's only living sibling at the time. Auntie never, as far as I can remember, explicitly taught me that God lives—that blessing came from my Sunday School teacher at our church. When I was a young kid, that church introduced me to the stylings of an evangelical preacher, who I will call "Pastor," and is where I came to know of God as a powerful being and was first baptized, at the tender age of seven.

> *The Holy Spirit that was described in this sermon was not the ethereal thing that caused convulsions I could not control, as I had witnessed in my younger years, but a renewal of life!*

Pastor permanently influenced my life through his revelrous presentation of gospel messages. Dancing and singing praises to God became the way I worshipped. What Pastor and all the other adults in my life failed to teach me, however, was how to have a personal relationship with God.

I saw people "slain in the Spirit"[1] and praying to God, but it all seemed like something that happened to people, not something I could individually initiate. Though I didn't know I could approach God directly, I believed in Him and wished to Him occasionally (I was never taught specifically to pray) about my desires through a rough childhood.

Between the ages of seven and fourteen, life was a continuous turn of pages in hell, with heaven sprinkled in at times. Hard were the years. Psychologically damaging were the years. But eventually, the mind-splitting abuse, privations, and other hardships eased and ceased, and the scars of those years started to mend.

I kept my faith in God through all of it. I wished to Him through the hard times, as any good follower would. I learned the rote prayers:

> *Now I lay me down to sleep.*
> *I pray the Lord, my soul, to keep.*
> *If I should die before I wake,*
> *I pray the Lord, my soul to take.*
> *Amen.*

Prayers, as I understood them, were memorized sayings. If anything else was taught to me about prayer, I failed to learn it. I gleaned that communication from God—being slain in the Spirit—was something that happened to you, and it had yet to happen to me.

One night, as a young teen of fourteen, I heard a sermon preached at church by a visiting pastor who stormed the pulpit, reminding me

---

1. "Slain in the Spirit" is terminology used by some religions to describe the experience when an individual collapses as they are completely overcome by the power of the Holy Spirit, wherein they lose all physical energy. Examples in the scriptures and Church history can be found in: Ezekiel 44:4; Matthew 17:1–7; Joseph Smith—History 1:15–18. The Church of Jesus Christ of Latter-day Saints does not officially use this term.

of my beloved Pastor! The familiar cadence in his voice quickened the familiar and opened my heart to a new feeling—sharp understanding!

It was as if the words this preacher spoke surgically entered parts of my soul, cutting away the scales of darkness in my life! Jesus Christ spoke of His words being this way, sharper than a two-edged sword, slicing with sharpness in all directions, as this man's words did to my doubt in Christ's power and divinity (see Hebrews 4:12).

Enthralled by the preacher's words, amid the cries of "Amen," excitement vibrated within me as he spoke of sanctification through Christ by the Holy Spirit of Promise. This preacher spoke of being children of Christ through sanctification. I knew I needed to become a saint.

His words spoke truth to my soul; the Holy Spirit manifested in me as it never had before. I knew this man's words were true. The Holy Spirit that was described in this sermon was not the ethereal thing that caused convulsions I could not control, as I had witnessed in my younger years, but a renewal of life!

Since this preacher was the first person to bear witness to my soul through the Holy Ghost of the truth of becoming a saint, I eagerly approached him following the meeting for further answers.

"I want to be a saint," I pleaded more than stated. "What do I need to do to become a saint through Christ?"

"You believe in Christ, right?" he offered. "You are already a saint."

My heart dropped, and my soul deflated. After all he had preached in his sermon about becoming new creatures in Christ, he did not have anything more for me than I already had! I felt numb.

"Make sure you buy a tape of my other sermons on the tables outside," he added, shaking my hand to conclude our exchange.

I did believe in Christ, but I still did not know how to worship or approach Him. I exited the church alone to gaze into the stars, out in full force that night, magnifying feelings of insignificance within. A strange mixture of fear, hope, and confusion rippled in surges through me as I regarded the peaceful stillness in the sky, the beauty of its endlessness. A desire to be there ignited within! I wished to end all the confusion and strangeness of life with the peace and calm of the night. Each star knew that it was a star and showed it brightly in the darkness. At that moment, I wanted to be with God and follow Him. Everything seemed clear.

The burning feeling in my heart diminished as the memory of this night faded into the reservoirs of my mind, like all the other fairy tales adults told children to make life seem better.

At that time, the hard life that I experienced had psychologically begun to manifest, encouraging me to cut pieces of myself away; the first cut would be from the religion that had failed to protect me from all the abuse and horrors I had witnessed. I needed a change to discover who I wanted to become, and God met me where I was.

I learned about the Moors of northern Africa and wanted to make a connection with them, with Africa. In the high school library of my small town, I found a section about Moors and skimmed the titles. One book with a sky-blue cover stood out from the others, which I now know was misplaced. I took it off the shelf and beheld a golden man blowing a horn. It was called the Book of Mormon, though my eyes saw "The Book of 'Moor' Man."

Reading the book converted me back to Christ and Christianity. It was different and new. It was not the Bible, which I had largely given up hope on since it hadn't seemed to do anything for me up to that point. The Book of Mormon taught me that Christ was real and that it was okay to believe in Him and His teachings.

> *I needed a change to discover who I wanted to become, and God met me where I was.*

I wore that book out! I read it until it came apart. I never did officially return it to the library. I would sneak it into the library and hide it on the floor next to the section where I had found it. The cover was cracked and chipping off. I felt horrible. I later went back to replace the book with a new copy, but in the moment, I did not want to pay a late fee, so I lied that I had returned it weeks before the due date. We found it conveniently on the floor in bad condition. I still checked it out.

With no spiritual guidance, I still had not learned enough about the book to gain awareness of its true power to change lives—to change my life.

My cousin, in an unrelated turn, invited me to a dance at his church. I initially declined, having recently returned to Christendom and not desiring to ruin my experience by going to a dance featuring gospel music or risking seeing someone slain in the Spirit and it not being me.

> *Reading the book converted me back to Christ and Christianity. It was different and new. . . . The Book of Mormon taught me that Christ was real and that it was okay to believe in Him and His teachings.*

He laughed at my ignorance, explaining to me that regular music would be played at the dance. He also said there would be girls to dance with! I changed my mind. He then hesitatingly told me there would be White people. I changed my mind again.

"White people and Black people don't go to church together or dance together," I explained.

"It will be fine. It will be fun," he countered.

"Will there be Black girls there for me to dance with?" I questioned.

"It will be fun. You'll see. Just come with me," he said, still not answering my question.

He convinced me, and I went. There were no Black girls. But I had the time of my life dancing with the White girls. Following the dance, I pestered him to take me to another church dance. He told me I had to go to regular church before I went to another dance, promising to send missionaries to my home, which he never did. After pestering my cousin at every turn because I wanted to go to a dance again, he gave me the number to call missionaries to my house. I called, but they never came.

Deciding I was just fine reading the Book of Mormon at home anyway, I moved on, not knowing there was a connection between my cousin, that book, and his church. I had never heard of something called a "Mormon" or "Mormonism." I was all about Christ. Even at the dance, the only thing I heard about the name of the church was that it had to do with Christ, and that's it!

Then a documentary aired that opened a question in me: what if I had missed the true Church of Christ, or what if it had left the earth? Floored and perplexed again about life, I wanted to know if the true Church still existed on earth or if it had vanished altogether. I did not know what to do, still not having learned to pray. Even after reading the Book of Mormon, I still had not figured out that I could directly approach God. That book converted me to Jesus Christ, but I still had no introduction to Heavenly Father.

I struggled with some religious ideas. It made no sense to me that God and Jesus were the same person. It made no sense to me that we had no prophets testifying today. Where were our prophets? What a strange fruit I was, thinking those thoughts at fifteen instead of focusing on football and parties like my friends.

By March of 1992, at the end of my freshman year of high school, I was pining over my plight, wishing God would help me. Then the knock at my door came.

My mom and stepdad told me to tell the visitors to go away. I opened the door, and two big White guys stood before me doing what they called "tracting" in the area. I tried to tell them to leave but felt compelled to let them into the house against my parents' wishes. One particular elder had a sparkle in his eyes that I could not stop looking at—it was as though he had something to tell me, and he did!

It took a moment for me to get over the idea that important-looking

White people actually wanted to talk to me. White people lived around where we lived, but we understood that we were not supposed to deal with them regularly, so I didn't. I avoided White people unless I had to do business with them or if I was at school.

Once the two young men started talking about God and Jesus, I was ready for them to go. I already knew about God and Jesus. I believed in Them. But then the other elder started talking about prophets.

An alarm sounded, and my whole spirit listened. In my mind, I began to connect questions I had pondered to the things the missionaries were saying. I also noticed the word *Saint* in the name of their church. From that point on, no one existed but those two men; they opened the Bible and shared Amos 3:7: "Surely the Lord God will do nothing, but he revealeth his secret unto his servants the prophets."

As the other elder spoke, my spirit vibrated with excitement, and a substantial and peaceful feeling permeated the room and settled into my soul! If they told me about a living prophet, I would believe them and do whatever they wanted me to do! Excitement grew inside of me and took root in my bosom as I anticipated the next things they would say. My hopes were high. I had been let down by that preacher when I told him I wanted to be a saint in Christ, but I was certain that this would not happen again! I was not disappointed.

Elder Sparkle-Eye told me about Joseph Smith Jr.—that he was a fourteen-year-old boy seeking for truth about what church to join because he was confused about religion.

My heart leaped within me! Joseph was just like me, a seeker of truth; except I was fifteen years old, not fourteen. We read the account of Joseph Smith, who went into the woods to pray for the first time vocally. I had never prayed in earnest before. This boy Joseph did right to pray.

In James 1:5–6, I read, "If any of you lack wisdom, let him ask of God, that giveth to all men liberally, and upbraideth not; and it shall be given him. But let him ask in faith, nothing wavering. For he that wavereth is like a wave of the sea driven with the wind and tossed." Joseph took James's advice and prayed.

As Elder Sparkle-Eye recounted what Joseph Smith had reported happened to him, time seemed to stand still, and all creation became reverent so that I could hear with my whole soul! In answer to his prayer, God the Father and Jesus Christ appeared to him.

> *As the other elder spoke, my spirit vibrated with excitement, and a substantial and peaceful feeling permeated the room and settled into my soul! If they told me about a living prophet, I would believe them and do whatever they wanted me to do!*

I could not speak. My soul seemed to leave my body because my heart learned what it felt all along was true. My body felt a rich, gentle heat that consumed me with love and pure understanding. My ears grew warm, and my mind was experiencing the vision with Joseph! I went into another world of pure joy as God answered the longing of my heart. A mere boy had seen Him and His Son together, verifying in my mind what I had assumed! God still reveals Himself to people, even children! My astonishment was so great I could not contain myself! I did not feel to shout or scream. I did not feel to dance. Joseph's experience overcame and subdued me in reverence.

Elder Sparkle-Eye asked me to accept baptism. I immediately said yes. I knew they were true messengers of God. They talked about the Book of Mormon and were surprised that I was already familiar with it. The rest of the meeting was like a dream. Joseph Smith was a prophet of God!

Elder Sparkle-Eye told me afterward not to believe it just because he said it. "Ask God," he encouraged, "to let you know personally, without us here."

After they left, I went to my room and knelt in the middle of the floor. Even though I believed in God, I had never purposefully prayed before about anything. I knelt just a bit away from the door and asked God in all sincerity of heart if He was there.

The most peaceful feeling surrounded me, as if embracing me, as the word YES filled my heart and mind with knowledge and power—but more. Tears came quickly. I remember how I felt. The exquisite joy and love are hard to describe, though I have since had many experiences to know that feeling as the Holy Ghost's confirming influence.

No longer did I feel uncertain about God's existence, because He had revealed Himself to me. It changed my life. I was just a fifteen-year-old boy who did not know how to pray, but He still answered me in my heart and in my mind. God revealed Himself to little me!

Elder Sparkle-Eye baptized me on March 29, 1992. I later served a mission in the South Africa Cape Town Mission from December 1998 to December 2000. I met and married my wife afterward, and we were sealed on May 12, 2001, in the Atlanta Temple. Seven children later, that supernal experience in my childhood bedroom has never left me and fills me with the Spirit each time I think on it. The Spirit slew my doubt; so finally, I had been slain in the Spirit. It was something that had both happened to me *and* had been initiated by me.

> *I went into another world of pure joy as God answered the longing of my heart. A mere boy had seen Him and His Son together, verifying in my mind what I had assumed! God still reveals Himself to people, even children!*

"AS A MOTHER IN ISRAEL, THOU SHALT BE KNOWN AMONG THE PEOPLE"

JANE ELIZABETH MANNING JAMES
1821–1908

Jane Elizabeth Manning James was born in Wilton, Connecticut, to Philes and Isaac Manning. Her mother had been enslaved but was freed by the time Jane was born. Little is known about her father. Following her baptism in 1842, Jane received the gift of tongues. Church records indicate that this was not a singular incident; she exercised this gift throughout her life, as minutes of Relief Society and Retrenchment Society meetings in the late nineteenth century document. Jane's compassion and charity were well known: in April 1849 she gave half of the flour she had to the White American family of Eliza Partridge Lyman so they would not starve, she cared for her ill son for approximately ten years, and even though they were separated, she cared for her ailing husband, Isaac Manning, until he died. She was known as Aunt Jane by everyone and is one of the best-documented and most well-known Black American members of the Church. Her death made front-page news, and her funeral was well attended; Church President Joseph F. Smith spoke at her funeral. Although allowed to enter the sacred temple to perform proxy baptisms, she was denied entrance to receive her personal higher ordinances.[1] On July 22, 2022, a new statue of Aunt Jane was unveiled and dedicated by President M. Russell Ballard at This Is The Place Park in Utah.

---

1. See "Journal of Eliza Maria Partidge Lyman," https://mcqueenfamilyhistory.files.wordpress.com/2016/06/journal-of-eliza-maria-partridge-lyman.pdf, 20–21: "April 8th, 1849. . . . We baked the last of our flour today, and have no prospect of getting any more till after harvest. April 25th, 1849. . . . Jane James, a colored woman, let me have about two pounds of flour, it being about half she had." See also Sherilyn Farnes, "'We Cannot Sit Down Quietly and See our Children Starve': An Economic Portrait of a Nineteenth-Century Polygamous Household in Utah," in Business and Religion: The Intersection of Faith and Finance, ed. Matthew G. Godfrey and Michael Hubbard MacKay (Religious Studies Center, Brigham Young University; Salt Lake City: Deseret Book, 2019), 197–228. https://rsc.byu.edu/business-religion/we-cannot-sit-down-quietly-see-our-children-starve; and "Quincy D. Newell, "James, Jane Elizabeth Manning,"

When a child only six years old I left my home and went to live with a family of White People. . . . I was raised by their daughter. When about fourteen years old I joined the Presbyterian Church. Yet I did not feel satisfied. It seemed to me there was something more that I was looking for.

I had belonged to the church about eighteen months when an Elder of the Church of Jesus Christ of Latter-day Saints was traveling through our country preached there. The pastor of the Presbyterian Church forbid me going to hear them as he had heard I had expressed a desire to hear them; but, nevertheless, I went on a Sunday and was fully convinced that it was the true Gospel he presented and I must embrace it.

> But we went on our way rejoicing, singing hymns, and thanking God for his infinite goodness and mercy to us, in blessing us as He had, protecting us from all harm, answering our prayers, and healing our feet.

The following Sunday I was baptized and confirmed a member of the Church of Jesus Christ of Latter-day Saints. About three weeks after while kneeling at prayer the Gift of Tongues came upon me, and frightened the whole family who were in the next room. One year after I was baptized I started for Nauvoo with my Mother Eliza Manning,[2] my brothers Isaac, Lewis, and Peter, my sisters Sarah Stebbings, and Angeline Manning. My brother-in-law Anthony Stebbings, Lucinda Manning, a sister-in-law, and myself.

We started from Wilton, Connecticut, and travelled by canal to Buffalo, New York. We were to go to Columbus, Ohio before our fares were to be collected, but they insisted on having the money at Buffalo

---

Century of Black Mormons, University of Utah, https://exhibits.lib.utah.edu/s/century-of-black-mormons/page/james-jane-elizabeth-manning#?c=&m=&s=&cv=&xywh=-2246%2C-183%2C6551%2C3656.

2. Ms. Jane's mother's name was Philes (pronounced Phyllis) Eliza Mead; after marrying Isaac Manning, Philes took that surname.

and would not take us farther. So we left the boat, and started on foot to travel a distance of over eight hundred miles. We walked until our shoes were worn out, and our feet became sore and cracked open and bled until you could see the whole print of our feet with blood on the ground.

We stopped and united in prayer to the Lord. We asked God the Eternal Father to heal our feet, and our prayers were answered and our feet were healed forthwith.

When we arrived at Peoria, Illinois the authorities threatened to put us in jail to get our Free Papers.[3] We didn't know at first what he meant for we had never been slaves, but he concluded to let us go. So we travelled on until we came to a river. And as there was no bridge we walked right into the stream. When we got to the middle the water was up to our necks, but we got safely across. And then it became so dark we could hardly see our hands before us, but we could see a light in the distance. So we went toward it and found it was an old log cabin. Here we spent the night. Next day we walked for a considerable distance, and stayed that night in a forest, out in the open air. The frost fell on us so heavy that it was like light fall of snow. We rose early and started on our way walking through that frost with our bare feet, until the sun rose and melted it away. But we went on our way rejoicing, singing hymns, and thanking God for his infinite goodness and mercy to us, in blessing us as He had, protecting us from all harm, answering our prayers, and healing our feet. In course of time we arrived at La Harpe, Illinois, about thirty miles from Nauvoo.

At La Harpe we came to a place where there was a very sick child.

---

3. "Free papers" were documents that declared the free status of Black American people during the enslavement period. They were issued by the state where the person resided. If a person did not have these papers on them when stopped, they could be arrested or sold into enslavement. It was not uncommon for a person's papers to be taken from them. For a sample of a freedom document/certificate, see www.loc.gov/exhibits/african-american-odyssey/images/02/0202001r.jpg. For more information, see Michael E. Ruane, "Lost Slave Freedom Papers Tell of the Tortuous Paths Out of Bondage," *Washington Post*, February 20, 2017; Christine Blackerby, "Kidnapping of Free People of Color," November 12, 2013, National Archives.

We administered to it, and the child was healed. I found after the Elders had before this given it up as they did not think it could live.

We have now arrived to our destined haven of rest, the beautiful Nauvoo! Here we went through all kinds of hardship, trial, and rebuff, but we at last got . . . directed . . . to the Prophet Joseph Smith's Mansion. When we found it Sister Emma was standing in the door, and she kindly said, "Come in! Come in!"

. . . Brother Joseph took a chair and sat down beside me and said, "You have been the head of this band haven't you?" I answered, "Yes, sir!" He then said, "God bless you! Now I would like you to relate your experience in your travels." I related to them all that I have above stated and a great deal more minutely, as many incidents have passed from my memory since then. He then said, "God bless you. You are among friends now and you will be protected." They sat and talked to us a while, gave us words of encouragement and good counsel.

We all stayed there one week. By that time all but myself had secured homes. Brother Joseph came in every morning to say good morning and ask how we were. . . . On the morning that my folks all left to go to work, I looked at myself clothed in the only two pieces I possessed, I sat down and wept. Brother Joseph came into the room as usual and said, "Good morning. Why! Not crying?" "Yes, sir. The folks have gone and gat themselves homes, and I have gat none." He said, "Yes, you have. You have a home right here if you want it. You mustn't cry. We dry up all tears here." I said, "I have lost my trunk and all my clothes." He asked how I had lost them. I told him I put them in care of [someone] and he had lost them. Brother Joseph said, "Don't cry. You shall have your trunk and clothes again."

Brother Joseph went out and brought Sister Emma in and said, "Sister Emma, here is a girl that says she has no home. Haven't you a

> *He then said, "God bless you. You are among friends now and you will be protected."*

home for her?" "Why yes, if she wants one." He said, "She does," and then he left us.

Sister Emma said, "What can you do?" I said, "I can wash, iron, cook, and do housework." "Well," she said, "when you are rested you may do the washing if you would just as soon as do that." I said, "I am not tired." "Well," she said, "you may commence your work in the morning."

The next morning she brought the clothes down in the basement to wash. Among the clothes I found Brother Joseph's Robes. I looked at them and wondered. I had never seen any before. And I pondered over them and thought about them so earnestly that the Spirit made manifest to me that they pertained to the New Name that is given the Saints that the world knows not of. I didn't know when I washed them or when I put them out to dry.

. . . I had to pass through Mother Smith's room to get to mine. She would often stop me and talk to me. She told me all Brother Joseph's troubles, and what he had suffered in publishing The Book of Mormon. One morning I met Brother Joseph coming out of his Mother's room. He said good morning and shook hands with me. I went into his Mother's room. She said, "Good morning. Bring me that bundle from my bureau and sit down here." I did as she told me. She placed the bundle in my hands and said, "Handle this and then put it in the top drawer of my bureau and lock it up." After I had done it she said, "Sit down. Do you remember that I told you about the Urim and Thummim when I told you about The Book of Mormon?" I answered, "Yes, Mam." She then told me I had just handled it. "You are not permitted to see it, but you have been permitted to handle it. You will live long after I am dead and gone. And you can tell the Latter-day Saints that you were permitted to handle the Urim and Thummim."

Sister Emma asked me one day if I would like to be adopted to them as their child. I did not answer her. She said, "I will wait a while and let you consider it." She waited two weeks before she asked me again. When she did I told her, "No, Mam." Because I did not understand or know what it meant. They were always good and kind to me, but I did not know my own mind. I did not comprehend.

Soon after they broke up the mansion and I went to my Mother. There was not much work because of the persecutions. And I saw Brother Joseph and asked him if I should go to Burlington and take my sister Angeline with me. He said, "Yes, go. And be good girls. And remember your profession of faith in the Everlasting Gospel and the Lord will bless you." We went and stayed three weeks then returned to Nauvoo. During this time Joseph and Hyrum were killed.

In all the Lord was with us and gave us grace and faith to stand it all.

I shall never forget that time of agony and sorrow. I went to live in the family of Brother Brigham Young. I stayed there until he was ready to emigrate to this valley. While I was at Brother Brigham's I married Isaac James. When Brother Brigham left Nauvoo, I went to live at Brother Calhoon's. In the spring of 1846 I left Nauvoo to come to this great and glorious valley. We travelled as far as Winter Quarters. There we stayed until spring. . . . In the spring of 1847 we started again on our way to this valley. We arrived here on the 22nd of September 1847 without any serious mishaps. The Lord's blessing was with us and protected us all the way. The only thing that did occur worth relating was when our cattle stampeded. Some of them we never did find.

. . . My children were all raised to men and women, and all had families except two.

My husband Isaac James worked for Brother Brigham. And we got along splendid accumulating horses, cows, oxen, sheep, and chickens in abundance. I spun all the cloth for my family clothing for a year or two. And we were in a prosperous condition until the grasshoppers and crickets came along carrying destruction wherever they went, laying our crops to the ground, stripping the trees of all their leaves and fruit, bringing poverty and desolation throughout this beautiful valley. It was not then as it is now. There were no trains running bringing fruits and vegetables from California or any other place. All our importing and exporting was done by the slow process of ox teams.

Oh how I suffered of cold and hunger. And the keenest of all was to hear my little ones crying for bread, and I had none to give them. But in all the Lord was with us and gave us grace and faith to stand it all. . . . I have lived right here in Salt Lake City for fifty-two years and I have had the privilege of going into the Temple and being baptized for some of my dead.

I am over eighty years old and I am nearly blind, which is a great trial to me. It is the greatest trial I have ever been called upon to bear. But I hope my eyesight will be spared to me, poor as it is, that I may be able to go to meeting and go to the Temple and to do more work for my dead.

> *My faith in the Gospel of Jesus Christ as taught by the Church of Jesus Christ of Latter-day Saints is as strong today; nay, it is, if possible, stronger than it was the day I was first baptized.*

I am a widow. My husband Isaac James died in November 1891. I have seen my husband and all my children but two laid away in the silent tomb. But the Lord protects me and takes good care of me in my helpless condition. And I want to say right here that my faith in the Gospel of Jesus Christ as taught by the Church of Jesus Christ of Latter-day Saints is as strong today; nay, it is, if possible, stronger than it was the day I was first baptized. I pay my tithes and offerings. I keep the Word of Wisdom. I go to bed early and rise early. I try in my feeble way to set a good example to all.[4]

---

4. Jane E. Manning James autobiography, typescript; Church History Library, Salt Lake City; used with permission from The Church of Jesus Christ of Latter-day Saints. The title of this essay is from Jane's second patriarchal blessing, given by Church Patriarch John Smith, dated 1889. Newell, "James, Jane Elizabeth Manning," Century of Black Mormons.

GIFTS OF GOD

ALICE FAULKNER BURCH

Alice Faulkner Burch was born in Oxnard, California, to Cleo and Elwanda Faulkner. A member of the Church for thirty-eight years, she has served in various callings including a full-time mission in the Chile Santiago South Mission (1987–88), ordinance worker in the Salt Lake Temple, and helper at the Utah State Men's Prison Family History Center. Living in Utah with her husband, she volunteers on several boards about Black American history.

I've always known Jesus Christ. That knowing made me a "strange" child and is the underlying of my "strangeness" now as an adult.

My first memory of knowing Him was as a child. I sensed a higher presence with me, watching over me and guiding me. Even as a child I knew things there was no way a child should or could know. There was always a voice whispering to me, telling me. To me it seemed natural that I knew these things.

I learned formal prayer from someone Mama was helping. Mama was always teaching, helping, and feeding someone. He taught me to kneel beside my bed, bow my head, and fold my hands together. He taught me to pray: "Now I lay me down to sleep, I pray the Lord my soul to keep." After that I knelt beside my bed every night. I had seen Mama sit quietly with her hands folded and her head bowed, but I never knew what she was doing until that night I was taught formal prayer. By the time I was a young teen, saying that rote prayer wasn't enough. I was talking with God all day, sharing the events of my day and my troubles and asking Him questions. There was so much to talk with God about!

Years later I learned that Mama had been the one who had taught that young man to pray. I asked her why she never taught me to pray. She said, "I didn't want you to feel pushed into religion. I didn't want you to feel that God was shoved onto you. If you chose that, then you chose it." I didn't know if I chose Him or if He chose me. I only knew the path felt right and that He continued with me.

> *I was talking with God all day, sharing the events of my day and my troubles and asking Him questions. There was so much to talk with God about!*

I don't remember how old I was when I had my first vision. In some manner visions and revelations have always been with me, always a part of me. From childhood to now, the veil between this segment of life and the first and next segments has been thin for me.[1]

Being brought up in Oxnard, California, I didn't grow up attending church. The majority of my "God education" came in our home in two ways: gospel music and Negro spirituals Mama played on the radio, TV, and records; and preachers she watched on TV. Oral Roberts. Billy Graham. Jimmy Swaggert. Pastor Frederick K. C. Price. Drawn to truth, I listened. Pastor Price was my favorite because he taught straight from the Bible. Being an avid reader, I comprehended what he taught well. I appreciated that he taught the Word with the energy of pure, strong faith that caused the Word to become part of my very being and settle in my innards.

As strong as the energy of faith was from Pastor Price, I felt it was

---

1. Visions and dreams as a form of spiritual communication have a longstanding foundation in Christianity and Restoration scripture. For instance, speaking of the last days, Joel 2:28–29 reads, "I will pour out my spirit upon all flesh; and your sons and your daughters shall prophesy, your old men shall dream dreams, your young men shall see visions: And also upon the servants and upon the handmaids in those days will I pour out my spirit." And 2 Nephi 4:23: "Behold, he hath heard my cry by day, and he hath given me knowledge by visions in the night-time." See also 1 Nephi 1:8; 8:2; 2 Nephi 26:13; Alma 19:16.

equally strong from a short White American man I heard briefly on the TV one summer day in 1984. It was the only time I ever heard him speak. Later I learned the man was Spencer W. Kimball. By the time I attended my first general conference, he was no longer speaking due to the throat cancer that had taken his vocal cords.

We had a large Bible in our home that Mama read often, leaving notes throughout. From time to time I picked it up and read her notes. Some were questions; others were verses she had copied with "Remember this one" written really big at the top. Often I turned to the verses she had written down and read them. I was drawn to the Bible. I felt an energy of light emit from it.

In July 1984 I had a several-day spiritual experience. Swept away in the Spirit and spiritually ministered to, I was told the keys to identify the Church of the Lamb upon the earth. At the close of the experience I arose, told Mama I had a phone call to make (which was inappropriate because I always had to ask), found the phone number of The Church of Jesus Christ of Latter-day Saints in Oxnard, and called. The man who would be my first bishop answered. I told him I was calling to have missionaries come prepare me for baptism. The next day I answered the door to two young men who said, "We're missionaries from The Church of Jesus Christ of Latter-day Saints. We received a phone call that Alice asked for us to come by."

"Yes!" I responded happily. "I'm Alice. You're here to prepare me for my baptism?"

They looked at each other wide-eyed, then stammered until they found their words: "Um, we want to set up an appointment." And so we did.

At each appointment Mama was present, making sure nothing bad happened. On my first Sunday, I walked into a chapel that I had never been in, and it felt familiar. One of the hymns we sang in the sacrament meeting was "O My Father," a poem torn from a book I had found many years earlier. I had picked up the page and read the poem.

It had touched something deep in me of familiarity and home and eternity and invited me to remember. I kept that page and read the poem so often that I had memorized it. As a young adult, it comforted me that my "strangeness" was actually "divinity" by its true name. So it was that I knew the words to the hymn, to the shock of those Church members sitting next to me.

> *For a wise and glorious purpose*
> *Thou hast placed me here on earth*
> *And withheld the recollection*
> *Of my former friends and birth;*
> *Yet ofttimes a secret something*
> *Whispered, "You're a stranger here,"*
> *And I felt that I had wandered*
> *From a more exalted sphere.*[2]

On Saturday, July 14, 1984, I was baptized. When the missionary who had taught me lowered me into the water, I felt buried; when he raised me, I felt a newness of life enter me and saw my feet set on a path to walk hand in hand with Jesus. That night I was shown a vision: I was in that space seeking God's church, but I didn't feel the past confusion. I knew which door to go to, and I did. When I opened it and stepped into the room, it expanded and soon I stepped from the water and walked across a shore to where Jesus sat. No one told me the man was Jesus. I knew because He felt as He had always felt: filled with light, exuding light, even though He sat

> *I felt a newness of life enter me and saw my feet set on a path to walk hand in hand with Jesus.*

---

2. "O My Father" is a poem written by Eliza R. Snow in 1845; it was first published in the *Times and Seasons* in Nauvoo, Illinois. Its original title was "My Father in Heaven." *Times and Seasons*, vol. 5 (November 15, 1845): 1039.

quietly. He said only one simple sentence to me as He took my hand: "I'm so pleased you chose to follow me."

That night the Holy Spirit informed me that there was more to be given me.

I have known Jesus since I was a child. I have known the intonation of His voice and the feel of His presence. My first bishop in the Church explained my experiences to me. That was the day I understood my "strangeness" through the eyes of God: He had bestowed spiritual gifts upon me.[3]

Through the thirty-eight years of my membership, I have been given many other gifts of God; some only for a short time as I served in a calling or during a particular situation, while others have stayed with me since the time I received them.

Jesus has always stayed with me. Even during times when people I loved turned their backs on me, I was physically and verbally abused, members told lies about me, local leaders eschewed me, a gift of wrapped dog poop was left for me, letters were sent to me telling me to leave the Church because I didn't belong, threats to kill me were made, and the unsuccessful attempts to harm me. Jesus has always stayed with me, blessing me and teaching me and reassuring me.

In August 1987 I entered the Salt Lake Temple and exited endowed with power from on high, a step closer to the complete fulfillment of what the divine voice told me when I was promised that there was more to be given me than what He had yet given me.

I believe in the gifts of God—those spiritual gifts that come to us

---

3. See Doctrine and Covenants 46:8–9: "Seek ye earnestly the best gifts, always remembering for what they are given; for verily I say unto you, they are given for the benefit of those who love me and keep all my commandments, and him that seeketh so to do; that all may be benefited that seek or that ask of me." And 3 Nephi 29:6 reads, "Yea, wo unto him that shall deny the revelations of the Lord, and that shall say the Lord no longer worketh by revelation, or by prophecy, or by gifts, or by tongues, or by healings, or by the power of the Holy Ghost!" See also Romans 11:29; 1 Corinthians 12:3–5; 14:1.

from a loving Heavenly Father via the Holy Spirit. I believe that they are given to us to strengthen our faith, to bless one another, to testify of the validity and existence of God and Jesus the Christ, to help us through difficulties, to uplift the entirety of the membership body of the Church, to assist and bless others, and to remind us that our time here certainly isn't all there is to life. I believe that the gifts are still here. I believe that every member of the Church can have the gifts we need to excel in a calling, to be patient in affliction and tribulation, and to endure to the end. I believe because we are the crowning creation of our God, and because it is part of His plan for Jesus—the Lord of this earth—to do all He can to help us be successful here.

> *I believe because we are the crowning creation of our God, and because it is part of His plan for Jesus—the Lord of this earth—to do all He can to help us be successful here.*

The spiritual gifts I've been given, the years I've been here, the opportunities I've received, and the walk I'm taking with Jesus have all been gifts from God as well. Members often ask me *why* I joined this church and *why* I've stayed a member. It's difficult to explain with mere words, but I tell them as best I can. It's my birthright to receive all the ordinances, and my being in this church is *my* walk with Jesus.

SPIRITUAL LEARNING AND SOCIAL BELONGING

JERMAINE SULLIVAN

Jermaine Sullivan was born and raised in Tuscaloosa, Alabama. He is a barbecue enthusiast, a prolific melody maker, and a lyricist. He is a returned missionary and a former bishop and stake president. Jermaine is a licensed professional counselor in private practice. He currently lives in Atlanta, Georgia, with his wife and three sons.

It has now been more than twenty years since I entered the waters of baptism and made a sacred covenant with God to keep His commandments and stand as a witness of His reality "at all times and in all things, and in all places that [I] may be in" (Mosiah 18:9). It has been, and continues to be, a personal journey filled with the full range of human emotions: joy and self-doubt, peace and fear, gratitude and insecurity, zeal and anxiety. Through the years my faith in the Lord Jesus Christ has sustained me, so much so that I've felt imbued with the courage to face my challenges and consequently experience personal growth.

My first year as a member of the Church was filled with deep gospel learning after what felt like an extended period of deep gospel longing. I had visited so many churches and offered so many prayers seeking spiritual clarity, that when I was introduced to the doctrines and practices of the Church, I knew I had found my place, my spiritual home.

> *"Yes, there are many differences between you and these, your brothers and sisters, but your common testimony of Jesus Christ will help you find unity, peace, and fellowship."*

Although the Lord had blessed me with the religious and spiritual clarity I was pursuing, I was increasingly aware of an unpleasant internal dissonance caused by a troubling juxtaposition: I was grateful for the enriching experience of soul-satisfying spiritual learning but was unsettled by my weak sense of social belonging. The Lord recognized my uneasiness and quickly taught me a spiritual lesson that was indelibly written on the "fleshy tables of [my] heart" (2 Corinthians 3:3).

I recall being at a Wednesday-evening Church activity with a group of young single adults. I had been more inclined to participate in these activities on previous occasions, but that night I wasn't up to it. I stayed in the background, lost in my thoughts. A doubt-filled internal dialogue began. I started to wonder whether I really belonged in this church. "Seriously, though, maybe I'm just too different," my internal voice said. I observed that I was one of only two Black people in the whole building. I felt like an incongruous dash of pepper on top of a pile of sea salt. Was the kindness many of them showed even real? I didn't think anyone had intentionally done anything to make me feel unwelcome. In fact, I had never met a more welcoming group of people. The bishop was particularly attuned to his sacred role as shepherd of his flock. Yet I was still challenged by the mental disharmony of feeling spiritually at home but socially and culturally miles apart from my fellow Latter-day Saints. It was the sobering reality that differences can create distance. I was very close to leaving the activity and fully reconsidering how I would conduct my spiritual walk before the Lord.

At a certain point in all this mental wandering, a penetrating and timely sunray of thought found its way through my otherwise overcast state of mind: "Jermaine, these are your brothers and sisters." These words came into my heart and mind with fresh meaning. It felt like a curtain was pulled back, allowing me to see and feel and hear a new truth that had been, until then, hidden and muted.

As these sacred impressions lingered with me, it was as if the Lord was saying: "Jermaine, I have brought you a long way. I have spared your life. You have sought the truth, and I have revealed it to you. This is your new pathway. Don't leave. This is your new home. Yes, there are many differences between you and these, your brothers and sisters, but your common testimony of Jesus Christ will help you find unity, peace, and fellowship."

My mind was filled with clarity! I felt like the Apostle Peter, who when faced with the decision to stay or leave, responded with one of the shortest but perhaps most profound testimonies on record: "Lord, to whom shall we go? thou hast the words of eternal life" (John 6:68). In some ways, faith in Jesus Christ bestows the ability to know in part but do in full. I was more willing at that moment to give my full heart to the journey of discipleship, notwithstanding my very partial knowledge of what staying would mean for me socially and culturally. I found it strange that while the room was alive with activity, conversation, and laughter, I was in the middle of a life-altering exchange with heaven. This sacred, spiritual experience taught me that I am "graven . . . upon the palms of [His] hands" (Isaiah 49:16), along with my fellow Latter-day Saints. Since that time the Lord has taken me on a journey of continued personal revelation and given me the honor of priesthood leadership.

> *In some ways, faith in Jesus Christ bestows the ability to know in part but do in full. I was more willing at that moment to give my full heart to the journey of discipleship, notwithstanding my very partial knowledge of what staying would mean for me socially and culturally.*

From the beginning of my discipleship, the Lord has often aligned people and events in ways that would benefit my eternal well-being. Applying His infinite foresight on my behalf, the Lord lovingly aligned my plans to move to Atlanta, Georgia, with the call of a particular missionary, and that elder's family with an intelligent, surprisingly still single, Ugandan convert.

Douglas Shaw was called to the Alabama Birmingham Mission, which included my hometown of Tuscaloosa, Alabama, where he and his companions taught me the gospel of Jesus Christ and baptized me into the Church. Elder Shaw was from Atlanta, where I would soon be moving to attend school. Kembe Nakiina, who would become my wife, grew up in the same ward as Douglas. He and his father, George Shaw, arranged for me and Kembe to meet up at the North Point Singles Ward, adjacent to the Atlanta Georgia Temple. We became friends and officially started dating on August 29, 1999.

One evening after a few months of getting to know each other, Kembe surprised me by boldly inviting me to pursue two life-changing goals, which she expressed with an unbelievably straight-to-the-point conciseness: "You should serve a mission, then come back so we can get married!" I was stunned by her unflinching candor but was very much open to both these goals. I hadn't even been a member of the Church a full year and didn't know the first thing about the process of becoming a missionary. Nonetheless, I started praying to know if it was God's will for me to pursue full-time missionary service. I received an undeniable answer from the Holy Ghost in the same way He spoke to me before: my mind was filled with clarity, and my heart swelled with what felt like an uncommon sense of peace. It happened just as Kembe had envisioned. I served a mission in Fortaleza, Brazil, from 2000 to 2002. After I returned home, we were married on May 16, 2003.

One of our first decisions as a married couple pertained to where we wanted to live and worship. After prayerful consideration, we looked for housing within a certain ward's boundaries, a mostly African American ward located in southwest Atlanta. I had become aware of the ward after speaking to a group of youth shortly after receiving my mission call. Kembe and I felt that being part of the Atlanta ward would give us the sacred privilege of assisting in building up the kingdom of God among Saints with a familiar culture and experience. We felt guided to combine our consecrated efforts and talents and our hope, faith, and prayers with theirs in the work of salvation. It was in that ward that I became aware of the faith-filled lives of pioneer African American Latter-day Saints. It was there that I witnessed Black and White ward members submit, as a holy offering, sincere efforts to create gospel-rooted racial harmony as they served together, prayed together, and rejoiced together. I had the unanticipated privilege of shepherding that sacred work while serving as bishop of that Atlanta ward from July 2006 to April 2012.

The Lord surprised me again by giving me the privilege of serving as president of the Atlanta Georgia Stake from June 2012 to June 2021. In that sacred role I sought to promote unity among Saints of diverse cultural, racial, and linguistic backgrounds.

Ultimately, my life has been a tale of unexpected becoming.

I pause to recall with new understanding a particular evening in my youth when I lay on my bedroom floor while tears streamed down my face. I was highly anxious and depressed. I wondered what I could possibly do with my life since I wasn't a great high school student. I wondered if I would ever find someone to love. I prayed earnestly for God to show me a way forward and how to mend my brokenness. Now I see that in that moment of sheer weakness, God already saw the person I would become, the person I am still on a journey of becoming. He saw a baptism, an eternal marriage, and the raising of three sons. He saw the pursuit of an education. He saw beyond my imperfections to grant me the privilege of priesthood service. On my path, He has guided me carefully around sharp curves and carried me with His might up steep hills. I am grateful for His continued providence and watchcare, and for giving me a sense of eternal belonging among my spiritual kindred.

> *I witnessed Black and White ward members submit, as a holy offering, sincere efforts to create gospel-rooted racial harmony as they served together, prayed together, and rejoiced together.*

SPIRITUALLY LOCKED AND LOADED

RAH FREESTONE

Rah Freestone is a certified life coach, writer, and speaker. She was born in Kansas City, Missouri, and raised in Topeka, Kansas. She has a bachelor's degree in human development from the University of Kansas and two master's degrees (in managing organizations and creative writing). Rah collects scarves and enjoys morning walks, thrifting, and puns. She lives with her husband and their blended family in Kearney, Missouri, and dreams of serving a French-speaking couples mission (to Paris, of course).

I am a Black woman. I am a Christian. I am a disciple of Jesus Christ. I am a woman of faith. I am a kingdom woman. I am a child of God. I am your sister.

The journey to who I am today has been paved by many religions. I have been influenced by spiritual teachers and leaders, both family and nonfamily, formally and informally, directly and indirectly.

The women who came before me were deeply spiritual. They were praying women who handled the role of matriarch with dignity while also accepting a deep sense of patriarchal responsibility due to necessity. For many years, my grandmother Shirley was celebrated on Father's Day. From her life circumstances, she was instilled with a strong dependence upon God.

Such lessons from my childhood have remained with me, building the understanding that I now have to recognize and reverence all that is sacred.

Last fall, I spoke at my grandmother's funeral. In my remarks I shared her legacy counsel, which was this scripture: "Seek ye first the kingdom of God, and his righteousness; and all these things shall be added unto you" (Matthew 6:33). This is what she repeated to us all as a guiding principle for our lives. She constantly sought God's kingdom, and in her seeking through various religions, she eventually found The Church of Jesus Christ of Latter-day Saints and became our family's pioneer member.

As the lead spiritual mentor in my life, Grandmother Shirley influenced me on both physical and spiritual planes, and at another level I cannot begin to describe. To me, she is like Mother Eve.

> She was there from the beginning.
>
> She named me.
>
> She is the Mother of All Living.
>
> She is our Grand Mother,
>
> a blessed Matriarch for generations.
>
> She taught me the meaning of numbers
>
> and signs and symbols.
>
> She endured ridicule on her journey to Truth.
>
> She elevated my reverence for Womanhood.
>
> She is every Woman before me.
>
> She is in me.

My mother and father grew up attending parochial school in the heart of Kansas City, Missouri. It wasn't until I was much older, and it had been pointed out to me, that I realized how properly they spoke for people from the "Midtown KC 'hood." Catholic schools were a foundation of their upbringing and thereby influenced mine.

Home life was a little different during my early childhood years. When my mom practiced Buddhism, I remember sneaking to open the doors of her laminate altar box but knowing not to touch the sacredness inside. Such lessons from my childhood have remained with me, building the understanding that I now have to recognize and reverence all that is sacred.

While attending Faith Temple Church of God in Christ (COGIC) and St. Mark's African Methodist Episcopal (AME) in Topeka, Kansas, I paid attention with earnest interest to what it meant to catch the Holy Ghost, partake of symbolic bread and grape juice, and to send praises to Jesus out loud—especially in song.

Hymns and Jesus music have taken many forms over the past four decades, but the church song that stirred my little soul the deepest and earliest was "Let There Be Peace on Earth." Its lyrics taught me that there can be peace, and I can be a starter of its ripple effect. I sang "Kumbaya, My Lord" at every youth camp gathering. I sang "Let There Be Peace on Earth," the Unity Church theme song, at nearly every meeting we had. Both songs worked within me as positive affirmations, simultaneously strengthening me and pulling me toward my spiritual potential.

Attending the Unity Church was the humble beginning of the development of my spiritual roots. From ages three to seven, I learned from a metaphysical[1] Christian perspective. It laid the foundation for my familiarity with spiritual things. The big ideas that are hard to explain were made simple for my young mind to grasp. It was the founding of my kumbaya attitude, which celebrated every child on

---

1. Metaphysical: "Derived from the Greek *meta ta physika* (after the things of nature); referring to an idea, doctrine, or posited reality outside of human sense perception. . . . Metaphysics is a type of philosophy or study that uses broad concepts to help define reality and our understanding of it. Metaphysical studies generally seek to explain inherent or universal elements of reality which are not easily discovered or experienced in our everyday life. As such, it is concerned with explaining the features of reality that exist beyond the physical world and our immediate senses. . . . Metaphysics might include the study of the nature of the human mind, the definition and meaning of existence, or the nature of space, time, and/or causality." "Metaphysical, Faith and Reason," PBS, accessed September 28, 2021, https://www.pbs.org/faithandreason/gengloss/metaph-body.html.

earth as my brother and sister in God's great family. With the habit of meeting and communing with people of various ages, races, ethnicities, orientations, and religions, it just made sense to me. As a result, I internalized the power to proclaim peace.

It was also where I learned that there is a difference between the spirit child of God I was first born as (*the Great Me*) and the flesh/natural man/ego (*the little me*) that likes to take over with its negativity and pride. It's where I first learned the power of the words "I am" in speaking and sharing myself with others, and that peace on earth begins with the Great Me. The most important connection I eventually made, however, was that the gift of agency enables me to choose between the two me's.

Although most of my young school days were spent in public school, my sister and I spent some time in private school. During my years at the Lutheran school in my hometown, I received a solid taste of schoolwide chapel devotionals once a week—bullying, crushing on a White boy, the French language, praying in the classroom (especially during Desert Storm), and religious discrimination after our family was baptized into The Church of Jesus Christ of Latter-day Saints. We left the school shortly after our conversion.

> *When I turned eight and was baptized, I made a covenant with God to follow the example of Jesus Christ and become the Great Me I knew and believed I could become. Since then, I have been on the covenant path to becoming more and more like Him.*

When I turned eight and was baptized, I made a covenant with God to follow the example of Jesus Christ and become the Great Me I knew and believed I could become. Since then, I have been on the covenant path to becoming more and more like Him. I am doing my part to establish an eternal family made of Great Me's.

The experiences of attending Pentecostal, Methodist, and Baptist churches and a Lutheran school and witnessing Buddhist in-home altar worship helped me develop a deep love for others, inner peace that permeated outward, and sensitivity to threats against peace. All of this was necessary for fulfilling my personal mission in life and achieving my spiritual potential.

Many of those threats against peace took place within my past marriages. When I discovered my first husband's indiscretions, bitterness grew between waves of desire to forgive. At the height of my hope that peace was possible, he died.

Widowed, my rebound second marriage took my innocent children through a short-lived but painful trip across the country. When my then-husband's abusive behavior led to my homesickness, morning sickness, and eventual miscarriage, I was conflicted but relieved as I accepted the Lord's will for us as a family.

My current husband and I strive together to honor our temple covenant to teach, guide, and bring blessings upon our blended family.

A study of Doctrine and Covenants 98 revealed just how far-reaching the effects are to continuously choose the peace of the Great Me: "If men will smite you, or your families, . . . and ye bear it patiently and revile not against them, neither seek revenge, ye shall be rewarded; . . . And these three testimonies shall stand against your enemy. . . . And then if thou wilt spare him, thou shalt be rewarded for thy righteousness; and also thy children and thy children's children unto the third and fourth generation" (Doctrine and Covenants 98:23, 27, 30).

I have been blessed. I'm grateful for all that I have learned and all I continue to learn on this spiritual journey. Every step along the way helped me to arrive where I am today, with the abilities and skills needed to refocus my eyes on Jesus so that I arise when I start to sink and get up when I stumble (see Matthew 14:22–31).

My religious background and strong ancestral foundation are where my emotional and spiritual resilience came from.

I am a Black Woman.

I am a Christian.
I am a Disciple of Jesus Christ.
I am a Woman of Faith.
I am a Kingdom Woman.
I am a Child of God.
I am Your Sister.

Can't nobody tell me nuthin' about who I am, because it's locked and loaded from within.

WHEN TRUTH FIRST SPOKE TO ME

When Truth first spoke to me?
It was in The Morning Sun
When Truth
First spoke to me.
Not in a voice
Flowery
Or sweet
Or wispy like The Cloud.
It was
Firm
Solid
Tangible.
The most real thing
Ever I felt
Or saw
Or knew.
I felt the Universe then.
Not a Planet or a Star.
The entirety of what
The Universe is.
Other worlds
Of Life
Of Love
Of Music
Of Unity.
Of Priesthood unending.
Of Glory unending.
Of Light continuous.

And I . . .
I was part of
The All.
No more alone
Sullen
Wandering.
I was connected.
Part of The Connection.
I was who
The Plan
Was about and for.
It was in
The Morning Sun
When Truth
First spoke to me.
I haven't been the same
Since.
I am a new Me.
All my same pieces
But put together
Differently
Brighter
Awake
Aware.
Enlightened by The Great Wisdom.
Touched by The Truth.
Part of The Universe.
Knowing now.
Understanding.

—*Alice Faulkner Burch*

SEARCHING FOR MY HEAVENLY FATHER'S CHURCH

PEPPER MCCOY

Dr. Pepper McCoy has an academic background in psychology, counseling, interdisciplinary community-based social work research, and adjunct faculty experiences. She is heavily involved in community-betterment endeavors and serves as the director of a nonprofit organization. Her community service and activism efforts focus on social justice, equity, diversity, and inclusion of Black, Indigenous, and Persons of Color (BIPOC). She is also a voracious reader; mindfulness, yoga, and fitness enthusiast; and an avid sports fan. She has multiple adult children and seven phenomenal grandchildren.

Sitting with painstakingly erect posture, hooded eyes, and an occasional exaggerated sigh meant to convey boredom, my gaze drifted to the picturesque southeast panoramic view of rows after rows of gardened farmland. The scene included a massive woody backdrop of longleaf, loblolly, and spruce pine trees that bordered the northwestward side of the Kisatchie National Forest in north central Louisiana. Midday sunbeams covered the back porch. The yard and farm animals hovered together in the shade near the far fence tree line or just napped, including a peculiarly partnered no-name stray cat and dog. Depending on the wind direction, an occasional breeze that stirred the stagnant heat either carried a familiar nice smell of fresh pine, corn, and other garden vegetables or the not-so-nice whiff of cows

> *There was much already inside of me as a little child that was worthy to be saved, illuminated, and emulated by the adults around me—namely, the graciously and lovingly given infinite eternal light of the Lord, Savior, and Redeemer Jesus Christ.*

mingled with pungent hog-pen scents from nearly half mile away. The always-annoying flying insects were scarce for a change. It definitely would have been a good time to be playing and swinging down at the big oak tree.

Ouch! I knew I needed to pay closer attention to the hand that was rapidly undoing my plaits before my head got yanked off, as Momma had annoyingly reminded me for at least the tenth time already. Tearing up in defense and feeling even more sorry for myself, I whined, "But who could blame me today, Momma!"

It was certainly not the typical ritualized hair-tending process of hair washing, drying, and hot ironing that Momma religiously did for herself and my youngest sister and me every Saturday. No, this Saturday was much, much different because tomorrow was a very special first Sunday of the month. I'd thought about that day for a long time, but of course being just seven years old, the time hadn't really been that long. In fact, my oldest sister, sixteen years of age, couldn't seem to help herself from dramatically exclaiming, "Child, at your age, you're barely wet behind the ears." I guessed she would be for-sure-fire wrong about that tomorrow, because tomorrow I was getting baptized, and my ears were going to get plenty wet, both front and back.

As satisfied as I was with that thought, another tricky issue arose in my rapidly racing thoughts. Why was I getting my hair washed, dried, and hot ironed today if I was just going to get it wet tomorrow? That alone told me how special tomorrow was meant to be, but come Monday, I knew I would have to be ready to wear afro puffs to school all week!

It didn't take long that memorable first Sunday to understand why nearly all church members avoided the very front pews, except of course, for a few lively expected-to-be-seen-and-heard elderly deaconesses. I was literally sweating under the steady, sin-detecting, penetrating gaze of the lead pastor, associates, and the entire choir! Reverting to my shyness-buster go-to, I closed my eyes and pretended I was anywhere but there, front and center waiting to be led like a lamb to the baptismal font and washed free of my sins and cute new hairdo.

Such was the scary and exciting beginning of my spiritual journey. Unbeknownst to me at the time, by virtue of a divinely preordained physical birth, preceded by nearly a century of pastoral paternal grandfathers, faithful ministerial architects of the Baptist faith, I now aspired to be yoked; there was much already inside of me as a little child that was worthy to be saved, illuminated, and emulated by the adults around me—namely, the graciously and lovingly given infinite eternal light of the Lord, Savior, and Redeemer Jesus Christ.

Familial stories, especially from older siblings, suggest I demonstrated extreme adoration for my mother, unquestioned obedience to parental rules, and strived to exceed their expectations for household chores and education. This personality eventually led toward my collegiate participation in several sports, compliments of a full scholastic scholarship—the first scholarship awarded to an African American female student at the state's flagship university. As a youth, however, it was perhaps my ghastly fear of bugs and animals, as well as an innate inclination toward peacekeeping—a character trait that was refined amid frequent sibling skirmishes—that distinguished me as uniquely odd among my siblings. Interestingly, my earliest memory also suggests that I was strongly introverted. To me, our geographical isolation on the outskirts of town felt like a blessing, at least most of the time, because it afforded opportunities to just sit in the front yard and think, undisturbed by passing vehicles or neighbors, for hours or to play under a massive oak tree that was a short distance from the house.

Such was my temperament at the tender age of five years, as I sat in the nearly half-acre front yard early one morning, playing in the dirt and grass and occasionally looking up at the sky, the various animal-shaped clouds, and beyond. I was searching for God, as I occasionally did, playfully at first but then more seriously. That morning, in particular, I puzzled over how odd it was that I had not actually seen Him yet, although I had been told often enough by my faithful mother that He surely lived up beyond the clouds in heaven. Within memorable moments, I suddenly and distinctly felt and somehow knew Father God was really up there, and even more mysterious to me at the time, somehow, I knew He knew me—I could feel Him watching out for me.

In addition to recognizing there is a supreme, loving, ever-present Being, as a youth, I also seemed to have limitless faith that the Savior Jesus Christ truly lived, that the scriptures were words of God, and that God heard and answered my prayers.

Though particularly grateful for this spiritual quest for something I couldn't quite name, playing high school sports and eventually college sports regularly tested my religious and spiritual resolve. As did navigating a deeply racialized campus as a student of color and the repetitive encouragement by some peers to drink or smoke, though in general those vices never made sense enough for me to give them serious thought.

> *I suddenly and distinctly felt and somehow knew Father God was really up there, and even more mysterious to me at the time, somehow, I knew He knew me—I could feel Him watching out for me.*

Unexpectedly, spiritual reflections, heartache, and sadness during this time resulted in an unsettling crisis of faith. This was precipitated by an unusual change in pastoral leadership at my church, which created acrimony among the congregants as time passed. Multiple divisions took root, and previously devoted church members hurled vicious accusations at others or sometimes spitefully responded to similarly worded grenades from members they had once referred to as beloved brothers and sisters.

A chasm resulted, and the battle lines eventually extended beyond the physical church building and into the neighboring community.

Previously shared confidences became fuel to discredit someone else's opinion or, worse, to push the individual and their family out of the church entirely. It was beyond disconcerting and deeply troubling to discern and acknowledge that the faith and church I was baptized in—which still professed to talk of Christ and was supposed to be the "body of Christ"—did not actually live up to its professed beliefs. Shockingly, a few members in leadership, accused of misconduct, resorted to refuting the perfected divinity of the Savior in an attempt to rationalize their own human fallibility.

As a result, staying in the church of my youth became untenable—a disturbingly poignant realization at the time that felt emotionally, psychologically, and spiritually monumental! It was as if I had been blindly tossed overboard and lacked the ability to swim. No one I had come to know inside the church or in the immediate extended family had the answers I needed to stay afloat religiously and spiritually in the fractious faith I had once called my second home. I was in a disconcerting nowhere place I hadn't known existed.

Eventually, late one sleepless night, two dichotomic thoughts entered my mind. The first was a sudden and chilling prospect that the religious doctrine I knew, including the Bible, was false. The second was the realization that I needed to go and find my Heavenly Father's church. I wasn't one to avoid such a spiritual challenge; in fact, I welcomed it as a testament to my faith and love for my Heavenly Father and, therefore, resolved that very moment to find His church.

Immediately, I began attending different churches. Bolstered by youthful, boundless faith and athletically driven, headstrong tenacity, I entered church after church, accompanied by a cousin or a teammate or two who were curious about my quest. Although I lacked the ability to fully articulate or understand my hopeful pursuit of finding my Heavenly Father's church, I wholeheartedly believed Father God had a church and that He would have me be where the pure doctrine of Christ was taught and lived seven days of the week.

Accordingly, my companions and I would earnestly enter a new church sanctuary and proceed straight to the congregation. We would sit close to the middle so I could, with laser-like precision, observe both the ecclesiastical leaders and members during the worship service. Finally, nearing the close of the program, I would bow my head and fervently pray and ask Father God if this was His church and where He would have me to be. After receiving my answer, I would raise my head and eyes to my friends and, with resolve, shake my head no. This pattern of searching continued throughout high school, college, and into adulthood. I explored every church I could locate in the much larger city where I eventually married and raised a family.

It took nearly twenty years to find The Church of Jesus Christ of Latter-day Saints. Peculiarly, even though I deeply and profoundly absorbed the missionaries' teachings and embarked upon an epic self-study of the faith, I didn't readily embrace it as Heavenly Father's divinely endowed church. Instead I often battled incredulous feelings, wondering why I hadn't heard of this church or located it before. A search for rational answers stymied my progress time and time again, as internet searches yielded twice as much negative material than what I unexplainably felt in my being was the truth. I finally realized that the negative information didn't hold up to even basic scrutiny. And then it became clear that I was attempting to intellectualize a gospel that seemed too good to be true and yet had the spiritual depth and religious doctrinal insights I had yearned for. In all my questioning and reasoning, it finally dawned on me that I needed to more faithfully do as I had done for years—ask sincerely the very divine omnipotent source who had initiated my pursuit to begin with.

> *I wholeheartedly believed Father God had a church and that He would have me be where the pure doctrine of Christ was taught and lived seven days of the week.*

So shortly thereafter, on another very memorable first Sunday, I sat on a pew, flanked by my children on either side and my husband to my left. After the ward's patriarch bore a powerful and deeply heart-and-soul-felt testimony, and after months and months of frustrations, trying to make sense of things in my own way, I, with absolute faith, bowed my head. I fervently and tearfully, believing with a deep, deep sincerity, prayed to a Heavenly Father I knew loved me and asked Him if The Church of Jesus Christ of Latter-day Saints was His divinely restored, holy priesthood–guided church on the earth today and if it was where He would have me be. From the moment I uttered the heartfelt words, my soul stirred and a gentle, sweet peace mixed with joy descended upon me. Tears freely flowed, and as I raised my head, I knew His merciful answer had spoken directly to my soul and was spiritually undeniable. From that moment forth, it was as if I had never not known.

> *Within the divine covenant precepts of this faith, I can truly become like, know intimately, and commune with divinity, including the Holy Spirit, and thereby live a life of unconditional love, boundless faith, and limitless hope in spite of pain, disappointment, heartbreak, or betrayal.*

Today, twenty-eight years later, I have not wavered from that extraordinarily divine assurance and my personal, spiritual, revelatory, eternal, and loving conversion to the gospel of Jesus Christ. With gratitude, after the harder than hard and hurtful religious experience of my youth, I no longer lack the words to fully explain my soul-searing quest to find my Heavenly Father's church or what I found.

Living the gospel of Jesus Christ is synonymous with being one with and a literal disciple of the Lord Jesus Christ. Within the divine covenant precepts of this faith, I can truly become like, know intimately, and commune with divinity, including the Holy Spirit, and thereby live a life of unconditional love, boundless faith, and limitless hope in spite of pain, disappointment, heartbreak, or betrayal. The gift of the Lord Jesus Christ's loving Atonement miraculously affords me boundless opportunities to overcome sin and temptation. Moreover, finding the fullness of the gospel of Jesus Christ did not stop the lifelong journey of my soul to become a part of that spiritual realm and reality that is beyond our basic earthly existence, because, ultimately, I truly love and eternally want to be with Father God, the Lord Savior Jesus Christ, and the Holy Spirit with all my heart, might, mind, and soul.

BORN OF GOODLY PARENTS

WAYNE LEE

Wayne Lee was born in 1967 to Walter Perry Lee III and Gloria Jean Shedrick Lee in Mount Clemens, Minnesota. He and Muriel McIntosh were sealed in the Salt Lake Temple and have five children. A retired US Air Force captain with twenty-eight years of service, he has a bachelor's degree in film communications. He is currently the second counselor in his Utah ward bishopric.

I've been a member of The Church of Jesus Christ of Latter-day Saints for thirty-three years, having been baptized in my early twenties. When I first read the Book of Mormon, I felt a connection with Nephi when he said he was born of goodly parents (see 1 Nephi 1:1). I felt the same way about my parents. They raised me to be a good person, to read my scriptures, and to live a good life. I was blessed to have been born with the wisdom to follow the good advice of my parents, and so I worked to live my life in the way they taught.

At seventeen years old, after graduating from high school, I joined the US Army so I could receive money for college. Following basic training, I found myself in a strange place and on my own in Oahu, Hawaii. It was a fun place, but I wasn't hanging out with the right people. They weren't bad folks—just not the ones I needed at that time. I came to the conclusion that I needed to return to church.

Back home before I joined the army, I was a member of a Jehovah's Witness congregation. I knew there was a Kingdom Hall on Oahu; I always seemed to pass it no matter where I went on the island. But when I decided to return to church, I couldn't find it. I did, however, pass a building that had a large white statue of Jesus Christ in front.

At this time, I was going through a rough period, and I wanted to talk to my mom and get her advice. But I couldn't call collect at this time, so I thought I would have to get through this on my own, alone. After driving around a bit, it got late, and I decided to pull over and climb into the back seat. I thought to myself, "I wish I could talk to Mom." I went to sleep and had a dream that I spoke to my mother. It felt so real that I was disappointed when I opened my eyes and she wasn't there. A few days later I got a letter from her saying she had a dream about me a few nights before but couldn't understand it. She said she couldn't help me since she was too far away, but she said the one person who would help me was Jesus and that I would get my answers through Him.

This letter from my mother confirmed what I had been feeling and what I needed to do. How did she know what to say to me in that letter? I knew she felt something from her dream, prayed, and immediately wrote me. I have never forgotten that feeling of the Holy Spirit I had while reading her letter. I believe in the power of a mother's prayer.

I then knew what I had to do. I had to go to church. I drove around Oahu looking for the Kingdom Hall once again but still couldn't find it. Instead I kept going past the Christus statue. The statue was located on the campus of Brigham Young University–Hawaii.

> *A few days later I got a letter from her saying she had a dream about me a few nights before but couldn't understand it. She said she couldn't help me since she was too far away, but she said the one person who would help me was Jesus and that I would get my answers through Him.*

A couple of weeks later, I went to a dance on campus in the evening. I met a group of young people about my age (nineteen-year-olds) who were fun to be around. They were from all around the world, but what impressed me the most about these young people was that they had a strong testimony of Jesus Christ. One of these friends introduced me to the missionaries. They all had a huge part in sharing the gospel with me and, more importantly, in being examples of how to live it.

After I got out of the active army, I was baptized on August 3, 1988. Almost two years later, on July 27, 1990, I entered the Missionary Training Center in Provo, Utah, to begin my two-year mission in Salt Lake City. After completing my mission, I met my wife, Muriel, and we were sealed in the Salt Lake Temple. We loved Salt Lake City and decided to raise our five amazing children here. We have been so blessed.

After almost thirty years, I was honored to retire from the air force as a captain. My military experience and my membership in the Church have allowed me quite literally to bear my testimony around the world. Currently, I serve as second counselor in my ward bishopric.

If you let Him, the Lord will work a mighty miracle in your life.

I have lived a full life. I have remained a member of the Church because the Lord has continued to bless me. Muriel and I are not perfect, but together we have been goodly parents to our children, like Lehi and Sariah were to their children and like my parents were to me. We have taught our children how to best live the gospel of Jesus Christ, and they have continued to be an abundance of joy to us.

This gospel is true. If you let Him, the Lord will work a mighty miracle in your life. I know He has in mine.

WHERE HEAVENLY FATHER LED ME

ESTHER M. BRANCH

Esther Branch was born in 1944, has been a member of the Church for forty-one years, and resides in Virginia. She graduated from the celebrated Armstrong High School, noted for developing many accomplished African Americans, and later graduated cum laude from Virginia Commonwealth University with a bachelor of arts degree in English. She was baptized in July 1981. Esther has one son, three grandchildren, and two great-grandchildren.

As I look back over my life, I realize just how blessed I have been. I have been able to see more clearly than ever the hand of Heavenly Father as He has guided me along and prepared me. I believe that Heavenly Father is our personal tour guide through this mortal life, and if we get out of our own way, we will understand that and experience many wonderful blessings. My great blessing came when I was baptized into The Church of Jesus Christ of Latter-day Saints. It is no coincidence that I became a member of the Church. I can see clearly how I was prepared and led by Heavenly Father.

At the age of ten I was baptized into my family's church. I vividly remember the night of my baptism: I cried for a long time. I didn't know why, but I felt weird. As a child, I received many revelations, which I didn't understand until much later in my life. I know exactly where I was and the time when many of these spiritual experiences occurred. My first revelation came when I was a very young girl of twelve or thirteen. I was standing in my backyard with nothing particular on my mind. It was a beautiful, bright day. For some reason I looked up at the sky. As I did, I distinctly heard a voice (many say it was a feeling or an impression—perhaps, but it was a voice to me). The voice said, "You are going to bring your family together." I did not think about this until after I joined the Church. Then, at first, I thought the message was about my earthly family. I soon understood it was about both those on the earth and those beyond the veil. I learned my mission was genealogy; I had been chosen to do the work for my ancestors.

Another spiritual experience came when I was an adult in 1967, when my son was three months old. His father and I were not of the same religion, so we were of differing opinions concerning baptism. His father wanted my son to be sprinkled in his church, and I wanted him to be blessed in my church. I didn't have any strong opinions on the subject of sprinkling; I simply wasn't comfortable with it. Since I remained fervent against the sprinkling, my husband called in the "top guns"—his parents—to intervene. I wasn't aware of their coming, so their arrival took me by surprise. His father was chosen to be the spokesman since he and I were close. After I let him have his say, I opened my mouth not knowing beforehand what I was going to say. The words just flowed from me: "No, my baby boy will not be baptized in your church. He will be blessed in my church and when he is of age, he will choose his own religion no matter what it will be. And I will be very upset with anyone who would try to persuade my son's decision." I left the room shaking, not from fear—but from the words I had spoken; they had come from my mouth but not from me. In line with my determination, my son was blessed in my family church. For the day of my son's blessing, I asked the minister to preach a special sermon for my son since I was giving him back to the Lord to use in His service. I

> *I believe that Heavenly Father is our personal tour guide through this mortal life, and if we get out of our own way, we will understand that and experience many wonderful blessings.*

believe this decision was divinely inspired because my son would be the catalyst for bringing the gospel to me.

Peculiar events happened at the end of 1980. My new husband was suddenly baptized into what I thought was a strange church. He told me odd things, like "All Latter-day Saints are rich." He wouldn't eat certain foods and gave me a book with a section entitled "Ether," whose name seemed to me to mimic the book of "Esther" in the Bible—all of this made me think he had surely lost his marbles.

While my husband attended his newfound church, my son and I continued to attend my family church. Then one Sunday I felt impressed to attend church with my husband. He was completely dressed and ready to go first. He said, "You're going to make me late."

I told him, "It's okay. I'll go another time."

He must have felt something too because his tone changed as he said, "Go ahead and get ready. I'll wait."

I asked my son if he wanted to go to church with my husband.

He replied, "No, I'll attend when you do." When I told him I was going, he quickly said, "Then I'll go also."

Upon entering the chapel of The Church of Jesus Christ of Latter-day Saints, I felt that every eye was on me. Walking into a place so quiet felt strange; however, when I left, I felt as though I was walking on clouds; my spirit seemed to soar. That day my son surprised me by excitedly saying, "I want to join this church!" My husband told him that a person had to be taught by missionaries first. From that day forward my son did not attend any other church.

As my son's lessons progressed, I often asked him questions to make sure he understood what was being taught. One evening as I was getting ready for bed, he came running into my bedroom declaring, "I'm on fire! I'm burning up!" I asked him what was going on. He said he had been reading the Book of Mormon. I didn't know how to respond. Not long after this my son was baptized, in March 1981 at the age of thirteen.

I soon accepted visits with the sister missionaries. When they showed me a picture of the Apostles, I wanted to know where the Afro-Americans were. After obtaining an answer from their mission president, they told me that due to the curse of Cain (which was, according to them, black skin) there were no Afro-American men in upper leadership. I accepted it. Looking back on their answer, I believe Heavenly Father allowed me to accept their explanation because if I knew then what I know now, I would have never accepted their answer or joined the Church.

Singing had always been a very special part of my life since the age of five. When ward members discovered I sang, I was asked to sing for a sacrament meeting. I sang there, and then I was asked to join the ward choir. This of course meant I would be interacting even more with members and attending the Church. Following my solo in sacrament meeting, some of the choir members invited me to go with them to stake choir rehearsal. I auditioned for the Richmond stake choir and was accepted. I even became one of the soloists in the Richmond Mormon Chorale.

One Sunday, I was impressed not to ride with my husband and son to church. Having received confirmation that the Church was true, I told my husband that I was going to my family's church to tell the minister there I was leaving. I felt I had to do this because I would be leaving behind a large part of my family legacy. You see, my maternal great-grandparents were the organizers of my family church. Previously, they had been members of the largest church in the southside area of Richmond. They left it because it was a several-mile round trip and they wanted to worship closer to their home. So they organized a new church, which became the foundation of my childhood religious training. The principles of the true Church were not new to me. I learned from my mother eternal truths. The knowledge I gained at my family's church has since been magnified to me as a member of The Church of Jesus Christ of Latter-day Saints.

I wasn't afraid to talk to my minister. I knew it was the right step to take to move forward. The Holy Ghost was strong in the room when I told the minister I was leaving. Sunk down into his chair, he said to me: "The only problem I have with people leaving is that they never return and share what they've learned." I promised him that I would return and share with him. I did, but he didn't want to hear it.

A few weeks later, on Friday evening, July 17, 1981, I was baptized. What a wonderful, joyful time! The ward choir sang, and the chapel was full. In the events that ensued I was often reminded of what the Holy Ghost had revealed to me thirteen years earlier: it was necessary that my son be allowed to choose for himself.

> *Walking into a place so quiet felt strange; however, when I left, I felt as though I was walking on clouds; my spirit seemed to soar.*

After joining the Church, I spent many hours in the early 1980s gathering information from the family history center and the state of Virginia. I was doing this before genealogy was popular with many Afro-Americans. Before Ancestry and FamilySearch came on the scene, I spent hours searching microfilm and microfiche reels. I also looked through cemetery and other records to find needed information. The revelatory experience I had as a young girl has been fulfilled and come full circle as I worked to bring my family together.

During my forty-one years as a member, I have had many callings in the Church: Young Women secretary, Beehive advisor, Young Women president, chorister, Relief Society teacher, and now Sunbeam teacher. While each of these callings had their unique difficulties, the most challenging was as first counselor in the stake Relief Society presidency. I thought I might experience prejudice from the women in the stake because I'm Afro-American, but I never thought it would occur within the presidency! One person in particular made a point of treating me as though I didn't belong. She consistently made negative comments concerning me in front of others. It got so bad that the situation was brought to the attention of the stake presidency.

> *It has not always been easy to be an Afro-American in the Church, but I am learning how to ignore the pettiness and focus on the high prize.*

It has not always been easy to be an Afro-American in the Church, but I am learning how to ignore the pettiness and focus on the high prize. I have come to realize that I can't get back to my Heavenly Father and His Son, Jesus Christ, having ill feelings toward my White brothers and sisters, and neither can they if they have ill feelings toward me because I'm Afro-American. Maybe this is a piece of Heavenly Father's justice.

I look back at how I became a member, the spiritual experiences that led me to where I am now, my experiences as an Afro-American in the Church, and above all I know this with firm certainty: I am where my Heavenly Father led me to be and where I belong. My path has been challenging at times, but it has also been scattered with blessings so rich and beautiful. Heavenly Father has been in front of me to guide me, on my side to bear me up, and behind me to push me forward. I know with all my heart that I am in the true Church, the church Jesus organized—The Church of Jesus Christ of Latter-day Saints.

HOSANNA! HOSANNA!

ELIZABETH "BESSIE" RITCHIE ROGERS
1884–1970

Elizabeth Ritchie Rogers was born to Nelson Holder Ritchie (a Black American man born enslaved in 1840 in Missouri, whose parents were a White American man and a Black American enslaved woman) and Annie Cowan Russell (a White American woman) on November 17, 1884, in Great Bend, Kansas. Ms. Bessie said of her father: "Father was one of the pioneers of Great Bend, Barton County, Kansas and helped in settling Great Bend. At this time the prairies were over-run with buffalo and he saw them shot down by the hundreds. He got started in business here and was one of the richest men in the county. He owned the largest hotel, livery stable, bus line street car line pulled by mules, and the hack line which was pulled by horses.... Father was a self-made man, having no schooling, but was able to keep all his accounts and records without error. He could add numbers in his head faster than the rest of us on paper." Of her mother, Ms. Bessie noted: "Mother was a great horse woman." The family owned two houses: the Big Pink House and the Little House (as they were well-known by). It was in the Little House that Ms. Bessie was born "among the trees and flowers," she said, and "where [she] lived with beauty everywhere."[1]

Ms. Bessie was baptized and confirmed at the East Bountiful Mill Pond north of Salt Lake City, Utah, on March 28, 1893. She married and was sealed to Willis Rogers on January 13, 1904, in the Salt Lake Temple. They made their home in Grayson, Utah (renamed Blanding in 1916), and had ten children together: nine boys and one girl; two sons died tragically. Following the death of her second son in 1920, Ms. Bessie turned to writing letters to other grieving parents; by 1963 (forty-three years after her two-year-old's sudden death) she had written over 1,900 letters. Her husband Willis passed in 1928, two years after the birth of their last child. Widowed, Ms. Bessie raised her children on her own, never remarrying.

Regardless of her and her children's Black American ancestry, all of her sons received the priesthood and all of her children received all temple ordinances well before June 1978. She devoted the remainder of her life to family history and temple work, becoming a worker in the Salt Lake Temple,

---

1. Elizabeth "Bessie" Ritchie Rogers, "History of 'Bessie' Ritchie Rogers," Century of Black Mormons, accessed August 2, 2022, https://exhibits.lib.utah.edu/s/century-of-black-mormons/page/rogers-elizabeth-bessie-ritchie#?c=&m=&s=&cv=&xywh=-358%2C0%2C1106%2C564.

completing genealogical research for over 1,000 deceased family members yearly, and creating a compilation of her family history into approximately twenty-seven volumes.

Ms. Bessie spent the remainder of her life in Salt Lake City, Utah, and passed in 1970 at the age of eighty-five years.

We were living at East Bountiful when the time came to dedicate the Salt Lake Temple. I was glad I was eight years old so I could go to the dedication. Father, Olive and Alvie went one day to the dedication and mother and I went the next day. Oh, that was a wonderful time for me in the Temple.

When we reached the top room where the dedication prayer was given, I heard the most beautiful singing I have ever heard. It sounded like thousands were singing. I jumped up from my seat and looked around and I could not see anyone singing. I said to mother, "Where is that singing coming from?" Mother said she could not hear any singing. I said, "Oh, just listen, it sounds like thousands of them." Then mother said, "Be quiet and listen to the singing, you are talking out loud." I did be quiet and listen to those thousands singing their praises to the Lord. And how they did sing! Hosanna! Hosanna! to the Lord and their voices went higher and higher. The singing sounded to me like it was coming from outside the Temple.

After it was over we found out it was the angels doing the singing and not everyone heard it, just a few and I was one of those few.

As we went on through the Temple I saw the Prophet Joseph Smith sitting in one of the rooms we had to pass. He was with a beautiful lady and some little children. I started to crawl under the ropes that were along the hall and said to mother, "Come on, lets go in and sit down, there are two chairs we can sit in." Mother grabbed me by the arm and said, "I can't see anyone in that room." When I saw the Prophet Joseph Smith in

> *I heard the most beautiful singing I have ever heard. It sounded like thousands were singing.*

that room he was a better looking man than any picture of him I have seen. I was not the only one that heard that wonderful singing of those thousands and saw the Prophet Joseph Smith. These things are as clear and plain to me today as they were the day I saw and heard them in the Salt Lake Temple at the dedication. I am 67 years old while writing and copying this and I still see and remember these incidents like they were yesterday."[2]

---

2. From the "History of Elizabeth 'Bessie' Ritchie Rogers," Memorial by descendant Kurt Rogers, Century of Black Mormons, accessed August 2, 2022, https://exhibits.lib.utah.edu/s/century-of-black-mormons/page/rogers-elizabeth-bessie-ritchie#?c=&m=&s=&cv=&xywh=-358%2C0%2C1106%2C564. Bessie Rogers was baptized on March 28, 1893 in Bountiful, Utah.

After forty years of construction, the Salt Lake Temple was dedicated on April 6, 1893, by Church President Wilford Woodruff. Many other persons reported hearing angelic and divine music and seeing non-corporeal visitors in the temple with the people who were present. President Wilford Woodruff said later: "The Heavenly Host were in attendance at the [first] dedication [service]. If the eyes of the congregation could be opened they would [have] seen Joseph and Hyrum [Smith], Brigham Young, John Taylor, and all the good men who had lived in this dispensation assembled with us, as also Esaias, Jeremiah, and all the Holy Prophets and Apostles who had prophesied of the latter day work. . . . They were rejoicing with us in this building which had been accepted of the Lord and [when] the [Hosanna] shout had reached the throne of the Almighty, they too had joined in the joyous shout" (in LaRene Gaunt, "The Power of God Was with Us," LaRene Gaunt), *Ensign*, March 1993.

THE ANSWER?
THE PLAN OF SALVATION

SHERRI CAMP

Sherri Camp is the genealogy librarian in Topeka, Kansas. A thirty-plus-year veteran genealogist, she has BAs in history and sociology and an MLS from Washburn University. She is the author of *African American Topeka*, founder and president of the Kansas Chapter of the Afro-American Historical & Genealogical Society (AAHGS), and the past President of AAHGS National. She is married with four children and six grandchildren.

There are several things that led to my conversion to the restored gospel. The first came from my mom. When I was a youth living in Kansas City, Missouri, my mom and I would have deep philosophical conversations about the universe and truth. She made sure that I learned the most important things in life, including how to understand and follow correct principles.

I attended various churches as a youth, under her direction and that of my great-grandmother. One church was the Unity Church of Christianity. They published *The Daily Word*, a booklet that came out monthly with scriptures and thoughts on principles from the scriptures and the books of great thinkers.

When we didn't go to Unity, we went to St. John's Baptist Church with my great-grandma Freda. I had my first spiritual experience there when I was twelve years old. I felt as though I was outside of my body, looking at myself. I still don't know what it was that happened to me, other than that I had what I called a "spiritual awakening."

At the time I was attending a Catholic school where I went to mass every day. We had religion classes in which we read a book called *Good*

THE ANSWER? THE PLAN OF SALVATION

News for Modern Man instead of the Bible. It was about Jesus but didn't have His words. All of this was very confusing to my young mind. But after my spiritual awakening, I was changed. It was like my eyes had been opened, and I could see things with a spiritual eye. I knew things that I hadn't been told. I could sense there was a presence in my life that was taking care of me. I felt the presence of my Savior.

After I left home in my early twenties, my mom gave me a book called *Melchizedek Truth Principles*, which set me on a path that led me to understand how true principles work in life. Before that I had been a rebel. I didn't believe in following society's norms or allowing them to control my life and how I lived. But after making many painful mistakes, I began to realize that there were principles that governed life and how to live it well.

> *After my spiritual awakening, I was changed. It was like my eyes had been opened, and I could see things with a spiritual eye. I knew things that I hadn't been told. I could sense there was a presence in my life that was taking care of me. I felt the presence of my Savior.*

I was twenty-four when I married the first time. We moved to Topeka, Kansas. When my husband passed away, I was attending Unity Church. I asked my minister: "What is death, and what does it mean?" He told me I needed a grief counselor. I knew that he meant well, but I was enraged. I couldn't understand why he didn't know what to tell me or what the answer was. I stopped going to that church, and I attended several other churches after that—both Pentecostal and Buddhist—because my mom was also investigating them. I was looking for answers to my questions about death and the spirit world.

It was then, in early 1986, that my mom had a dream about an angel blowing a horn. Later that year she visited a friend who was being taught by the missionaries. Being one who always wanted to learn, Mom also decided to meet with the missionaries. She was taught and accepted the gospel easily. There was just one problem: the Word of Wisdom. She was a two-pack-a-day smoker. But a miracle happened. The Spirit so enlightened her mind after reading Doctrine and Covenants 89[1] that she stopped cold turkey, never to smoke again! She said that if the promise in the scriptures was true—that the destroying angel would not have power in her life[2]—then that was exactly what she needed. She felt that the fire of lighting up cigarettes was like the fire of hell.

Shortly afterward, in the fall of 1986, she was baptized and I visited her in Wyoming. There she casually introduced me to the missionaries who "just happened" to come over for dinner. They didn't try to convert me but said if I had any questions to let them know. And of course, I had a question!

We discussed the spirit world and where my husband was and what death was. The conversation was so easy. I spoke to nineteen-year-old boys about things older, more experienced ministers couldn't and wouldn't discuss with me. That meeting was the only spiritual conversation I had with missionaries until months later.

After returning to Topeka, other missionaries came to visit me throughout the next six to eight months. (I would say Mom sicced them on me.) They were young kids, and they seemed nice. But after visiting the Latter-day Saint church for the first time in the spring of 1987, at the behest of my mother, I wasn't really interested. I felt out of place. Not because of my color: I was used to being in an environment where there were people of other ethnicities. But the Church members were so solemn. I visited church another time on my own without an invitation. When I went to a sacrament meeting, no one spoke to me.

---

1. This section contains the revelation known as the Word of Wisdom. Verse 8 reads, "And again, tobacco is not for the body, neither for the belly, and is not good for man, but is an herb for bruises and all sick cattle, to be used with judgment and skill."
2. See Doctrine and Covenants 89:21: "And I, the Lord, give unto them a promise, that the destroying angel shall pass by them, as the children of Israel, and not slay them."

THE ANSWER? THE PLAN OF SALVATION

I wasn't even acknowledged. I felt uncomfortable and got up and left before the meeting was over.

More experiences had to humble me before the right set of missionaries came on the right day in the fall of 1987, and my life changed forever. At the time, I was reading a book about the power of God. I strongly wanted to know about the power of God on earth, and I was searching for that power. It was then that I met "my missionaries." I didn't realize then, but before I knew it, I had found that power through the priesthood. And it wasn't until years later that I actually knew I had that power in the Lord's restored Church.

> *I strongly wanted to know about the power of God on earth, and I was searching for that power.*

My moment of true conversion came when I heard the missionaries quote the story of Joseph Smith's First Vision. I felt like I had seen Joseph experience his vision before I came to earth and that it actually happened just as he said it did. I saw it in my mind's eye, as if it were a video portrayal (even though I had never seen a video of the event). I knew that if Joseph Smith was a prophet, then the Book of Mormon was true and so was the Church. It was just that simple for me.

I never had the six missionary discussions. I was always asking questions. The answer I had been seeking to understand about what we are here to do in this life and where we went after death was the plan of salvation. I found the answers about where my husband had gone and about death—we lived with God before we came here, we have a purpose on this earth, and we will return to live with Heavenly Father again if we follow His plan for us.

One day the missionaries asked me if I wanted to be baptized. My response was: "I was wondering when you were going to ask me!" I was baptized on November 14, 1987, in Topeka.

I've had many growing experiences in the Church. My thirst

for knowledge and desire to learn and grow led me to desire all that Heavenly Father had for me. That meant getting my patriarchal blessing and preparing for temple covenants by learning about my family and interviewing my grandmothers. That's how I spent my first year in the Church.

Although I never thought much about being a Black woman in a White church, I did *notice* that there weren't any other Black or Hispanic people in my ward. I heard that those who did come once wouldn't return. I've felt the brush of racism, but I ignored it or attributed it to the ignorance of a specific person and not the group. I was more interested in the new knowledge I had found and how it was helping to make me the person I needed to be for me and helping me to teach my children what they needed to know to avoid the mistakes of life that I had made. Correct principles. That's what was important to me. They're what I focused on then and what I focus on now.

> *The answer I had been seeking to understand about what we are here to do in this life and where we went after death was the plan of salvation. I found the answers about where my husband had gone and about death—we lived with God before we came here, we have a purpose on this earth, and we will return to live with Heavenly Father again if we follow His plan for us.*

I wonder if I had had the gospel in my life from my youth if my journey would have been a bit easier. It is the dream of parents and grandparents that their children and grandchildren have a better lot in life: better experiences and more opportunities. That was my dream for my children, and now it's my dream for my grandchildren. I have seen that having the gospel in your life as a youth and living it opens doors of opportunities that allow more to be accomplished. The gospel provides more protection against the generational curses that seem to plague people.

How important it is for young women to be surrounded by those

THE ANSWER? THE PLAN OF SALVATION

who help them to remember that they are daughters of God and He loves them in a very real sense! It is essential they be taught and shown by examples from adults of varying ages to measure themselves by Heavenly Father's standards. This is what I often try to remind my own granddaughters, and I strive to model that for them so they have that example from me in their lives.

After searching for the truth over my thirty-plus years in the Church, I have added to my focus my people: my ancestors and my Black brothers and sisters. My desire to help my people has been ever present in my mind. I have found the best way to help them is to connect them with their family. Therein lies the spirit of Elijah[3] and the Holy Spirit, who teaches all things.[4] The connection to both my posterity and my ancestors has made all the difference in my life, for the world I live in now and the world to come.

> *Correct principles. That's what was important to me. They're what I focused on then and what I focus on now.*

---

3. See Malachi 4:5–6: "Behold, I will send you Elijah the prophet before the coming of the great and dreadful day of the Lord: And he shall turn the heart of the fathers to the children, and the heart of the children to their fathers, lest I come and smite the earth with a curse."
4. See Moroni 10:5: "And by the power of the Holy Ghost ye may know the truth of all things."

GOD WANTED ME IN THIS CHURCH

STUART SCOTT

Stuart Scott is a lifetime resident of Richmond, Virginia. After a term in Vietnam in US Army Security, he earned a BS in business administration and computer science. Having served as elders quorum president, stake high councilor, and branch president, he is now assistant communication director for the Richmond Coordination Council. He is married to Blanca Turitich-Jacquet, and they have one son.

I walked behind a large array of computer cabinets to look out a bay window, thinking about tomorrow. It had been nearly four years since they left Richmond, and I wondered what they would think if they knew about tomorrow.

What changed? What got me here?

It was late spring in 1981, and Virginia's humidity index was on the rise. I was in the master computer control room, the nerve center of the largest automated facility of its kind. The room was suspended several flights above floor operations. As usual, the deck below was ablaze with activity. But the chaotic pace seemed insignificant as I pondered the many events that now were obvious indications of God's plan for me. It was as if I were reading a road map backward; each marker was an indication that He wanted me in this Church more than I wanted to be in this Church.

The first time I had ever looked out this window was the first week of May 1973. The building was nearly empty—no people, only scattered equipment and crates of parts. I had exited the army on the last Thursday of April, applied for the job the following Monday, interviewed on Thursday, and started work the next Monday. The economy was weak, unemployment was high, and *scarcity* and *uncertainty* were the watchwords. Yet in my mind's eye, I had repeated manifestations that I would be employed in a room suspended from the ceiling of a huge building.

Now here I was in deep reflection about my life, pondering just how it had come to be that I was accepting baptism. That day, and many, many times since, I have contemplated the tender mercies extended to me that helped lead me to The Church of Jesus Christ of Latter-day Saints. I'll share a few.

> *I pondered the many events that now were obvious indications of God's plan for me. It was as if I were reading a road map backward; each marker was an indication that He wanted me in this Church.*

First was awaking from a nearly month-long coma. I had been very young, but I remember my mother screaming for help as I lay on the floor, regurgitating profusely and convulsing at the just-desegregated Woolworth's lunch counter. None of the White people present would help us. Uncle Mel told me all about how I had nearly died: "You a miracle boy! We prayed for you, boy! Protested at the hospital and at the city hall. White folks didn't care about Black children." Meningococcal meningitis had swept through our Negro section of town, leaving two dead and two comatose. "They claimed they didn't know what it was or where it was coming from," said Uncle Mel. "But we knew! All because the Black children had to walk across the city dump to get to school." Maybe it was a miracle that I had survived.

In our youth we have experiences that shape us. Some are edifying and some intimidating. Then there are those you never ever forget. Mr. Clark's eighth-grade Virginia history class was one I'll never forget. The school year was coming to an end. The last chapters of our Virginia history book were meant to prepare us for ninth-grade American history. One hot day (no air conditioning in those days!),

Mr. Clark elected to have us take turns reading aloud directly from the text. Following along as someone else was reading, we came to a paragraph accompanied with an illustration of a wagon train. The text read, "And Brigham Young took the Mormons west."

What happened to me next can best be described in the words of Joseph's encounter with James 1:5:[1] "Never did any passage of [text] come with more power to the heart of man than this did . . . to mine. It seemed to enter with great force into every feeling of my heart" (Joseph Smith—History 1:12). The words leapt from the page into me. What does an uncouth thirteen-year-old boy from the 'hood do with that? What's a *Mormon*?

That word revealed itself again years later while I was stationed in Alaska, the land of the midnight sun. Asked to give temporary accommodations to a young private, I okayed him staying in my room until rotations were completed. The private, a young Mexican from the brush woods of California, was unusual to me. Unusual because where I had come from, there were only Black people and White people. All that I knew about Mexicans had been shaped by Disney's TV show *Zorro*.

In the military, it was the norm to spend few emotional assets on anyone who could be shot, so I chose not to invest time in getting to know this kid. Besides, I knew he would be rotating out soon, likely to Vietnam. But I noticed that every night he had something to do or somewhere to go off base. I could never figure out how this kid had so quickly assimilated with civilians in Fairbanks, Alaska. What was his connection? He would come back talking about activities with peculiar names. And girls were always involved. His stories had a hint of church with something else added. One night we had a brief and abrupt discussion about his religion. Using terms unfamiliar to me, at one o'clock

---

1. James 1:5 reads, "If any of you lack wisdom, let him ask of God, that giveth to all men liberally, and upbraideth not; and it shall be given him."

in the morning with the full sun in my face, his conversation was boring until he said that he was a priest.

Zorro's infamous *Z* flashed across my mind. "You're no priest! Where are your robes and beads, dude? And why are you hanging out all hours of the night with girls!"

He said more, which raised little interest in my mind. I curled my legs in and was just about to pull up the blankets when he said something I could not ignore. "In my church, you can't be a priest. Black people can't be priests."

Avoiding the profane, I retorted, "When I want to be a priest, I'll be a priest. And no one will stop me!" As I buried my head under the covers to darken my vision, a curious feeling I had felt several times before welled up in me. *Did I just say that?*

Years later, and it was Tuesday, June 16, 1981. The next day I would be baptized. Out of nowhere a thought came that it had taken eight years for me to realize the obvious. These promptings and feelings were not happenstance.

Eight years ago, except for wires and boxes, this room was empty when the director of operations gave me a tour of the warehouse. I had just interviewed for the position of control room supervisor. Just before he opened the vault-like doors, I knew this was the place I had been envisioning. Once inside I walked directly to this window; the place felt familiar, and I knew then that the feeling had not been a phantom.

I recognize now that those impressions were not about the job. They were preparation for the truth I would be taught in this room. At times I had lived a rancorous, rebellious life, yet my core yearned for that elusive unbridled, self-evident truth. At one nadir of my meandering life, I actually promised God that if He showed me the absolute truth, I would . . . well, be careful what you promise God; He might be listening.

I thought again of the two men who, for at least two years, discussed religion with me. What would Bill and Nate be thinking right about now if they knew I was joining their Church? Where are they now? The engineering company that had the insulation contract for our materials-handling facility had a contingent of about twenty, mostly Latter-day Saint, engineers and computer techs. What should have been a two- or maybe three-year endeavor lasted nearly four years. Behind the scenes those folks took a ribbing about being Latter-day Saints. Some even blamed them for plotting the delays as sabotage against the world's largest cigarette factory.

I reflected over those years I had worked side-by-side with a battery of bright, intelligent people in a frustrating effort to get this facility running. Cigarette production was beginning in the main factory, and innumerable tests had to be conducted. Bill, Nate, and I were teamed together to conduct those tests. Bill and Nate covered the technical and engineering, and I, staging and execution. The process resulted in long wait times for staging, corrections, and repairs, which gave us plenty of time to delve into every—and I mean *every*—aspect of the gospel. They held nothing back and never treated me as an investigator. They shared with me all their knowledge of the gospel, from premortal existence to exaltation, from prophecy to seer stones, and from gold plates to revelation.

I recognize now that those impressions were not about the job. They were preparation for the truth I would be taught in this room.

We dove deeply into the priesthood-denial policy to the African diaspora. They both believed the tenets of their religion but were painfully conflicted about this policy, though they addressed it as best they could. They never gave me a Book of Mormon or invited me to church, but they did give me a copy of the Doctrine and Covenants. They questioned me, and I vigorously questioned them. We had great, penetrating discourses about all things religious. In the end, there was not one jot or tittle about the Church to which I had not been exposed.

They had been gone four years now. And tomorrow I would become a Latter-day Saint. Staring into the far distant nowhere, I felt grateful for the many other quirky things that were unmistakably pointers to the gospel: a fortuitous prompting about my life's direction, a revealing dialogue with a preacher, being removed from certain danger, special inspiration from a famous athlete, and many more events on the road map that led to my finding and accepting the gospel of Jesus Christ.

Since Bill, Nate, and the company left town, all that I learned lay dormant for a time. Or at least I thought so. Shortly after they left, I connected with two close friends, both African American. Walter, who I had known since childhood, and Earl Hunter Jr., who worked with me. Our three families were socially connected and occasionally traveled together. There was nothing unusual about that, except they had both had their own independent spiritual promptings that had changed their lives, and in the end, Earl baptized me and Walter confirmed me a member of The Church of Jesus Christ of Latter-day Saints. Independently, God had brought us each to where we needed to be and in so doing had also brought us together as brothers in the gospel.

I KNEW IT WAS TRUE

NORMA BANKS

Norma Banks lives in Kansas City, Missouri, where she was born and raised. She received her BA degree in communications from the University of Iowa. Having discovered sculpting, she focuses on improving her artistic ability and skill in order to increase her contribution of sending more beauty into the world. Norma is sixty-five years old and has been a member of The Church of Jesus Christ of Latter-day Saints since 1992.

My sister moved to Gaithersburg, Maryland, after her divorce to start over and raise her two children. I was living with her and was a single parent to my son. Her friend Linda lived down the street, and we noticed young men with suits and badges coming in and out of her townhome and immediately thought she was in trouble with the FBI or the IRS. One day my sister asked her into the house and told her we wanted to help her. We told her of our FBI and IRS theories. She burst out laughing and almost fell over.

"No," she laughed. "Those young men are members of my church, and they are teaching my husband gospel lessons."

We looked at her and said, "Oh, Bible lessons."

She said, "No. Book of Mormon lessons."

"What's that?" we both asked.

She then launched into a long story about Joseph Smith, gold plates, a vision of God and Jesus, and an entire history of the Church. Just when my sister started asking her questions, Linda said, "Sorry. I'm supposed to feed the missionaries. I have to go. I'll talk to you soon."

When my sister closed the door, I said, "If your friend believes all of that, she's crazy!" My sister just shook her head, but I could tell she was interested. Over the next few weeks she went over to her friend's house whenever she saw the missionaries and asked so many questions her friend's husband couldn't get a word in, and so they banned her from the townhome but promised to come teach her. She didn't think they would come. Boy, was she wrong! It was their job to teach others about the gospel.

My sister wanted to know more; she apparently wanted a degree in "Mormonism." But I wasn't interested; I thought we only needed the Bible for a reference point in life. I left the room each time they came, though sometimes I would join in prayer at the end. She was being taught three or four times each week.

Finally they taught her about the plan of salvation. They explained to her that her baby who had passed was with Jesus and that she would still have the opportunity to raise her. My sister's ex-husband was a Catholic who never went to church. When their baby passed away, the priest had told them the baby was lost. I had seen what that experience was like for her. After that lesson, she was all in and decided soon afterward to be baptized into The Church of Jesus Christ of Latter-day Saints. Still skeptic, I thought: "She was a Muslim for six months when she was a teenager. We'll see how long this church lasts."

She read the Book of Mormon every day and discovered new things each time to share with me. But I didn't want to hear it, so she stopped telling me of her discoveries. The big day of her baptism soon came. I went to her baptism and cried—something I never do. I thought it was because she looked so happy in the baptismal font. "Good for her," I decided. "Whatever makes her happy."

Then one day she came home from church, though it wasn't even Sunday. She had attended some Thursday meeting where they had taught her how to make chocolate candy. I decided that was it! She was turning into someone I didn't even know. Making chocolate! Who was she? A Stepford Wife? She was changing, and I didn't understand it or like it. I decided to take my son for a visit home to Kansas City and so bid her goodbye.

Things weren't ideal in Kansas City. It was good to see my mom, but I missed my sister. Out of my seven siblings, I got along with her the best. She was my best friend. While in Kansas City, I heard people make rude remarks about the Latter-day Saints, and I didn't like it because my sister was one. Not much time passed before I wanted to return to my sister in Maryland. She had always been the kindest and the smartest person in my life, and I decided to go back.

When I arrived at my sister's townhome in Maryland, the place was overflowing with Latter-day Saints because she had accepted an assignment as a "ward missionary." (The only "ward" I had ever heard of was Burt Ward, who played Robin on *Batman*, or someone being a ward of the state.) Church members were over all the time. These young men ate out of our refrigerator and mowed the grass. I felt relaxed and safe around them. They called me Sister Banks. One day while I was hurriedly making a sandwich before they ate up all the turkey meat, they asked me if I would like to take the missionary lessons. I said sure but immediately thought, "You're not going to change *me* with your words." My sister was hiding on the other side of the refrigerator and was ecstatic that I had agreed so readily.

Oh, they had no idea what a fight they had on their hands in the wrestle for my soul. What they were teaching me I already knew was true. I had figured out much from constantly reading from a young age. Plus the Spirit had taught me a lot because of my relationship with God. I knew He existed and loved me because I had met Him in my dreams when I was a sickly child struggling with asthma.

I always talked to Him and prayed to Him, although I thought He loved the people back in Bible times more because He had talked to them directly, walked with them on the earth, and given them prophets. That was the one thing that was stopping me from getting baptized—the lack of Black prophets. I knew without a shadow of a doubt we Black people were just as good as White people. If there were no Black prophets in the history of the Church, well then it couldn't be *His* church and I wasn't joining.

They asked me every week if I would commit to baptism, and every week I said no. After this had gone on for about six months, they told me they wanted me to talk to this very spiritual sister in the ward. I did, and she told me: "You must pray to Heavenly Father, and He will tell you all you need to know." The missionaries had read me the promise: "And when ye shall receive these things, I would exhort you that ye would ask God, the Eternal Father, in the name of Christ, if these things are not true; and if ye shall ask with a sincere heart, with real intent, having faith in Christ, he will manifest the truth of it unto you, by the power of the Holy Ghost. And by the power of the Holy Ghost ye may know the truth of all things" (Moroni 10:4–5). Somehow this sister said the same thing in a way that resonated with me, and I knew I had better pray to know for myself, but I still thought it wasn't where I belonged because of the absence of a Black prophet. I also knew that there was no answer that a *man* could give me that would satisfy the racial disparity that I knew wasn't of God. I was willing to pray, but I knew nothing would change.

One day I was in my son's room cleaning, when my Savior and Redeemer of the entire world declared to me, "This is my Church, and ye shall join." Jesus Christ came to me on earth and provided a hardheaded daughter with that supreme blessing that no one on earth could have given me. I trembled. I knew the voice of the Lord had spoken to me and that what He said was true. There, at the back of my mind, was the question that demanded a Black prophet. He knew. The Lord knew and said it didn't matter. I said: "Lord, if it doesn't matter to You, it doesn't matter to me." I walked back and forth with jubilation and awe at what had occurred. I stopped cleaning but could not keep still. I thanked Him over and over again for His consideration and kindness. I cried tears of joy that I had found the Lord's Church on earth!

I was so happy when I told my sister that I wanted to be baptized. I met with my missionaries, and they tiredly asked me the usual question—would I commit to baptism? Instead of my stock answer, I said yes. They couldn't believe it! It was a miracle. Once our joy settled into a comfortable feeling, they said they wanted to warn me of one last thing. They told me that there were individuals who were prejudiced in the Church and that I must pray for them individually because the Church was true. I told them: "The Lord of Hosts told me the Church was true, and I don't care if some members put on their white hoods, jump on their horses, and ride down the middle of the Church!"

> *My Savior and Redeemer of the entire world declared to me, "This is my Church, and ye shall join." Jesus Christ came to me on earth and provided a hard-headed daughter with that supreme blessing that no one on earth could have given me. I trembled. I knew the voice of the Lord had spoken to me and that what He said was true.*

I knew that this was the Lord's Church. And nothing and no one was going to stop me from being a member of it. On December 5, 1992, I was baptized. Over ninety people attended my baptism. My sister gave a talk. When I came out of the waters of baptism, she clapped her hands with joy.

"STEAL AWAY TO JESUS"

FINDING FAITH IN TRIALS AND PRESSING FORWARD

"These things hurt, but why would I keep on having faith in the Church? There is something that gives me courage. When I feel faint something lifts me up."

—*Ruffin Bridgeforth, founding member and first Genesis Group President*
1923–1997; baptized 1953

WHAT *ARE* YOU?

ANONYMOUS[1]

When I was forty-three years old, while helping my aged mother with her oxygen, she revealed that my recently deceased daddy was not my biological father. Instead, my biological father was alive and had been living about thirty miles away from me most of my life. And, oh, he was a Black man. That he was Black was somewhat significant since my whole family was White. Everyone. I had thought that included me. I had never been told or knew I was anything else.

Abruptly, I had changed ethnicities. But even though I hadn't known my true heritage up until this point, I had been forced to carefully and painfully navigate society in a particular way. My ambiguous features or my light-skinned privilege had not sheltered me from the realities of my unrealized actual ethnicity. My parents' lie had not kept me from living as a Black child, teen, or woman, but it had denied me the knowledge and support that could have helped me understand my experiences. Support from the Black community could have mitigated the animosity of my fellow classmates in school, who, I now understood, must have thought I was either willfully denying my race or incredibly stupid to not know who I was. Now that I had been let in on the hoax, I felt humiliated; it was a con that everyone around me had been aware of except for me, the ignorant dupe.

In 1976 my family drove to the Washington D.C. Temple to be sealed together as a family. The temple workers took my brothers and sisters one by one into the sealing room to be sealed to my parents. Separately they took me as well, and I was sealed to my parents. On a family trip to California in 1979 to visit relatives, my parents explained

---

1. The identity of this contributor is anonymous due to the sensitive nature of the story and to protect the family.

to me that there was an issue with my sealing paperwork, and I would be going to the temple to be sealed to them again. Just me. And so in 1979 in the Los Angeles Temple, I was again sealed to my parents. I didn't think twice about it. I was nine years old. I had no knowledge at that age of the Church's priesthood ban for Black men and ban for temple ordinances for anyone with even one drop of African blood. My parents had requested from the prophet in 1976 an exception, which had been denied. I could, however, be sealed "for time" to them, allowing my sham first sealing so that even my siblings would be unaware of my status. When the ban was lifted in 1978, my parents were able to truly have me sealed to them. I was clueless.

"What *are* you?" This question often greeted me before "Hello" or any introduction. Strangers stopped me in public to enquire about my heritage. This was not only annoying in its frequency but also in how it compounded my continual feeling of being "other." This otherness was obvious in various incidences. As a biracial Black woman who's lived in all sections of the continental US and in Hawaii, I've both learned and experienced racism and prejudiced behavior in vastly different and unique forms from people in all areas of the country. It pains me to say that I gave it as well as received it. My ambiguous appearance was a source of speculation and discussion in the small town in which I was raised, a distasteful presence to some of my brothers and sisters in the gospel, a pass for privilege, a justification for bullying in and out of the Church, and a front-row seat to the racism and hate discussed, both freely or with subtlety, and shared in my presence because I was assumed to be White or Latina or Pacific Islander or Asian or, as it turned out correctly to be, Black.

> *I follow the Christ, not man. Because I desire the blessings promised by Jesus. I seek truth confirmed by the Spirit. I knock to obtain testimony strengthened through Christ's tender mercies. I ask to have Christ's love with me constantly.*

WHAT *ARE* YOU?

When I was an adolescent, my father was assigned outside of our ward boundaries to be a branch president. As I grew into my teen years, I attended stake youth activities. My first was a stake Young Women camp. It became clear that the friends I had grown up with before being assigned to the branch were not interested in being my friends any longer. Worse, not only would no one sit with me or talk to me, but the girls at camp openly told me how nasty my hair was. I was so ashamed that I refused to take a shower when anyone else was around or get my hair wet or swim in the lake since there were no means at our primitive camp to tame my hair and not stand out. I was humiliated. Mortified. I never went to camp again or any youth activity involving outdoor activities or water. Never. Other stake activities were no different. I only continued to attend the youth dances and youth conferences due to an exceptionally dedicated Young Women leader who would take me and hang out with me.

My childhood doctor was also my stake president. He worked with my mom to keep me ignorant of my heritage while making sure that I received medical care specific to those with Black ancestry, like sickle-cell testing. He also aided in hiding my identity among local Church members when there was a priesthood/temple ordinance conflict. The stake patriarch, after meeting with my mother beforehand, agreed to not say anything in my patriarchal blessing that would reveal that I had African bloodlines. Learning this later, I felt my patriarchal blessing was fraudulent. I felt betrayed. Finally, in the 1980s, members of our stake donated blood to a BYU DNA project that offered results of our ethnicity for free. I never received my results. My mother later confessed that she had talked to the person taking my sample and told them not to inform me of results because I was unaware of my true ethnicity.

So many lies and consequences!

My biological father and I met in an emotional, welcoming reunion. He and his (my?) family were very kind. Curious about my extended family, I traveled with all of them to some family reunions. It was wonderful to share in the extended family's great desire to document and gather family history. Discovering information about my ancestors was exciting yet frustrating. The reality of the lost and undocumented history of enslaved Black Americans is infuriatingly sad. Even sadder for me were the gaps and holes in information I personally sought. The reality of these parent-child reunions is that they often do not grow into long-term relationships. After all, the parent who never chose to be in your life and their spouse who knew you existed and was okay not knowing you . . . well, they were okay with that for a reason.

After being hurt through exclusion from ordinances and collusion to maintain lies, why do I continue to be a part of The Church of Jesus Christ of Latter-day Saints? Because I follow the Christ, not man. Because I desire the blessings promised by Jesus. I seek truth confirmed by the Spirit. I knock to obtain testimony strengthened through Christ's tender mercies. I ask to have Christ's love with me constantly.[2] For every priesthood holder who negatively affected my life, there are more who have listened to the Spirit and been a boon and a blessing to me. I remind myself that, in my many imperfections, the Lord still reaches out to me to pull me up. Because He extends me that mercy, I try in my weaknesses, in my anger, and in my hurt to still extend mercy to others, including my parents. It's a process, to be sure.

> *For every priesthood holder who negatively affected my life, there are more who have listened to the Spirit and been a boon and a blessing to me.*

It would be disingenuous of me to say that I am not still affected by the discoveries and machinations that stripped me of my confidence

---

2. See Matthew 7:7–8: "Ask, and it shall be given you; seek, and ye shall find; knock, and it shall be opened unto you: For every one that asketh receiveth; and he that seeketh findeth; and to him that knocketh it shall be opened."

and my original image of my family. Some days I'm furious, deeply pained, and sorrowful. It will take time to heal.

So, who am I? I am simply me. I believe that we end up exactly with whom and where we are supposed to be to receive the blessings the Lord has for us and to be instrumental in being a blessing for others. I know I was given access to the restored fullness of the gospel so that I can do as much temple work for my Black ancestors as possible. So that they can have access to those saving ordinances that were denied them for so long. I know the Lord will provide a way for me to find them if I seek diligently and trust Him. If the journey to be and to become who He knows I can be is messy and even painful, so be it.

> *In my many imperfections, the Lord still reaches out to me to pull me up. Because He extends me that mercy, I try in my weaknesses, in my anger, and in my hurt to still extend mercy to others.*

What am I? Ultimately, I am a child of God. That's the identity I need to embrace most. I would not trade the beginning of my story or the journey of healing for the new blessings that blossom as a new picture of me is being created.

FROM TABERNACLE TO TEMPLE

KAYLA WYATT

Kayla Wyatt is an avid nature enthusiast who strives to connect others to nature. She lives in Oak Ridge, Tennessee, with her husband, three kids, hamster, and flock of chickens. She paused her wildlife biology studies in order to raise her family. She enjoys martial arts, camping, and date nights.

I never would have thought that a burning building could have represented me and my journey to the temple so well, but it did. Just like the Provo Tabernacle, I was raised up to be a good "building." I was active in the Church, even when my parents went through moments when they were not. I prayed, even after my dad left us and married someone else. I even dragged myself out of bed most days to go to seminary class. I grew up in the South and defended our faith every day, at least once a day. But things happened—Satan is always looking for opportunities to damage our faith.

Being a teenager is no joke. I eventually found myself in a toxic and abusive relationship for a little over two years. I felt like my spirit was screaming for help while my mind and body stayed chained to sin. Towards the end of our relationship, my boyfriend proposed to me. Many of my other friends from church were already starting to get married, and I felt pressured to do the same. But thankfully Heavenly Father stepped in.

After several dreams and promptings and counsel from many wise women, I broke off my engagement and decided to study abroad in

Japan. Before going, however, I decided that I was going to try my luck out West. A couple of weeks before going to Japan, I flew out to Utah, signed up for massage school, and found an apartment. I was all set to make the move to Provo, Utah, after my trip abroad.

After a life-changing time in Japan, I was back in Utah. I couldn't wait to be surrounded by temples, Deseret Book, and, most of all, single, good-looking guys who held the same beliefs as I did. I swore to myself that I was there to change. I was going to repent and be the holiest version of myself ever!

But instead, I got worse.

My weekly meetings with my bishop couldn't keep up with the unhealthy influences in my life. Those paired with the lack of mental counseling that I desperately needed to get over the trauma I had experienced threw me into a tailspin. I was sad, I was frustrated with myself, I was angry at Satan, and I often thought that I could feel and hear him laughing at me. I was desperate. I would often sit on the hill by the Provo Temple and just look at it, hoping that by some miracle I would one day be able to go into a temple again.

My prayers did not go unheard. After finishing massage school and moving across town to the apartments next to the university, I decided to fill my new free time with institute classes. I started going to as many classes as I could handle in a day and spent most of my time in the institute building. One day I saw banners for choir tryouts. I felt a strong prompting to try out, but I brushed it off. The prompting grew stronger throughout the day and stayed with me through work. The last customer on my shift randomly asked me if I could sing. I looked up at him in surprise and asked him why he was asking me that. He told me that the institute

> *Through Christ I found the redemption I yearned for. I found Him in ways that I never thought I could. He became the roots I have relied on to keep me anchored throughout the many storms that have come and will come my way.*

choir was having tryouts, and he felt like he should ask me if I could sing. I told him yes, I could sing. I had been in choirs since I was a little girl. He made me promise that I would at least try out, gave me a wink, and through the doors he went.

I was honestly very flustered and annoyed. Didn't God know that I was sick of choirs? I went home, threw my purse down, and angrily told my roommate that God wanted me to try out and asked if she could get her keyboard out to help me practice a song for the next day. She was a saint and helped me practice that night. I was chosen.

Things didn't magically get better for me, but I was now surrounded by spiritually solid friends, and we had an amazing director who taught us not only the songs we sang but also *about* the songs we sang. We were spiritually uplifted in every class. We performed with tears running down our faces as the Spirit flowed from us and around us. My journey with the choir came to a spiritual high as we prepared for our upcoming performance at the Provo Tabernacle with a prominent music composer known primarily for his film scores.

At the rehearsal, we began to smell smoke from where we were sitting in the upper seats of the Provo Tabernacle. I was one of the last people to leave the building after rehearsal, along with the show's soprano. I mentioned the smoky smell to several of the tabernacle staff before I left. The next morning I was awakened by a call from my cousin.

"Dude! The tabernacle is on fire!" she exclaimed.

I couldn't even make sense of what she was saying until I saw it on the news. It wasn't just on fire—it was blazing! The outside air was hazy from all of the smoke that came from the building. It was horrific.

About a month after the fire, I knew it was time to leave Utah. During my time there I had found a new love who I thought was worth fighting for, but I also knew that I had to leave him. I wanted to be temple worthy. I wanted an eternal marriage. I knew that I had to live away from him, so I moved back home.

Being back home was difficult and lonely. I knew that my main focus was to heal and to take the necessary steps to be able to be endowed and married in the temple, but Satan wasn't going to be kicked out without a fight. Every day seemed like a spiritual and mental battle. I got a job, took up various forms of partner dancing, and traveled frequently to fill the time. I also prayed more than I ever had before and met with my bishop regularly. As I clung to Jesus Christ and the words of the prophets, I felt as if I was snapping the flaxen cords that held me, one strand at a time.

> *As I clung to Jesus Christ and the words of the prophets, I felt as if I was snapping the flaxen cords that held me, one strand at a time.*

A year passed and I was ready to attend the Atlanta Temple. Complications with paperwork presented challenges, and my new fiancé and I weren't able to be married in the temple. The disappointment was crushing; nevertheless, we were married the next day and continued to spiritually grow together as we waited a year to be sealed in the temple.

I eventually got the eternal marriage I longed for, and through Christ I found the redemption I yearned for. I found Him in ways that I never thought I could. He became the roots I have relied on to keep me anchored throughout the many storms that have come and will come my way.

The Provo Tabernacle had also changed during that time. It became the Provo City Center Temple. Like phoenixes, we had both truly risen from the ashes.

Before our second child was born, my husband I visited family in Utah and were able to attend an endowment session at the newly formed temple. The session went well, but it wasn't until I was alone in the dressing room that the Spirit hit me hard. I began to weep. In that moment the Spirit showed me my past and contrasted it with my present. I was that temple. Like the tabernacle, I too had been something good. The tabernacle had burned and blazed and been stripped down past its foundation, and then it was made into something completely different from before—more beautiful and a place where the Spirit of the Lord could more fully reside. Through my own redemptive fires, I too had become completely new—more beautiful and a daughter of God in whom the Spirit of the Lord could dwell.

> *Through my own redemptive fires, I too had become completely new—more beautiful and a daughter of God in whom the Spirit of the Lord could dwell.*

NOT NECESSARILY FAIR

KEVIN FLOWERS

Kevin Flowers has been married for thirty-five years to Shelly Flowers. They have two children and live in Omaha, Nebraska. He graduated from the University of Nebraska at Omaha in business administration and from ICS Technical Institute in computer programming. He also has a master's degree in management from Bellevue University. Following service in the US Navy, he served a two-year mission in the Colorado Denver Mission. During his forty-three years as a member of the Church, Kevin has served in numerous callings, including Sunday School teacher, first and second counselor in the elders quorum presidency, branch president, and first and second counselor in the bishopric. He currently serves as a high councilor in the stake.

I was baptized on April 28, 1979, and have been a member of The Church of Jesus Christ of Latter-day Saints for forty-three years. I am happy to be a member of the Church. I believe that Joseph Smith Jr. was a prophet and he translated the Book of Mormon by the gift and power of God. I believe we have a living prophet today. I believe that if we live by the teachings of the prophets and scriptures, our journey in life won't necessarily be fair but we will have the strength to overcome this world as Jesus promised.[1]

In my life I have strongly focused on education to make sure that I am able to support my family, and I've also been blessed to serve in many callings. But regardless of all my education and the leadership callings I've held over the years, I have had many challenges to remaining a member of the Church. No number of degrees or callings can provide protection from racism or negativity. Like most Latter-day

---

1. See John 16:33: "These things I have spoken unto you, that in me ye might have peace. In the world ye shall have tribulation: but be of good cheer; I have overcome the world."

Saints, I thought of all Church members as a family that wouldn't hurt me. Discovering that was not always the case was like a blow to the gut. Yet I've pushed through the pain caused by racism and drawn strength from the Holy Spirit and grown my testimony. I have always remembered the feeling of the Spirit when He testified of the truthfulness of the gospel. That burning in my bosom has stayed with me and grounded me in the Church. But even with my personal revelations, I've struggled. To help myself stay focused on the gospel over the years, I've repeated these words over and over again: "The Church is true."

> *I believe that if we live by the teachings of the prophets and scriptures, our journey in life won't necessarily be fair but we will have the strength to overcome this world as Jesus promised.*

One of my first challenges was handling the uncomfortable feeling of being the only Black man in a building full of White people. It was hard. I felt that I was two people: one when I was around people of my own skin color and then another when I was around the White Church members. I felt like I was wearing a façade, which I hated. Having no one to talk to about this situation, I felt isolated. I turned to the scriptures and to prayer often to seek strength. Alma told his son Helaman to use the word of the Lord to guide his every step;[2] I've worked hard to do that.

Loving the gospel but struggling with interactions with members who have obvious bias toward me has been a tricky course to navigate. That bias has been varied. Some members have been curious, asking

---

2. See Alma 37:44–45: "For behold, it is as easy to give heed to the word of Christ, which will point to you a straight course to eternal bliss, as it was for our fathers to give heed to this compass, which would point unto them a straight course to the promised land. And now I say, is there not a type in this thing? For just as surely as this director did bring our fathers, by following its course, to the promised land, shall the words of Christ, if we follow their course, carry us beyond this vale of sorrow into a far better land of promise."

simple questions with obvious answers, since we're all human. Their questions reminded me of that simple query that sometimes comes from children: "Are you black all over like I'm white all over?"

As a young man, some Church members saw me as a threat, afraid that their daughters might date me and of what association with me would mean for them as a family, as "good, upright" members of the Church, and for their status in the area.

Once a Church leader spoke in our ward and said that members should seek a temple marriage and avoid dating nonmembers. In the same breath he told me and another Black brother we would have to date outside the Church to find a wife. I've had to cleanse myself of the impact that statement from a high-up leader had on me. Even so, my mind sometimes wandered back to it, laced with questions of my worthiness. White brothers were told to be faithful and keep dating within the Church because God would bless them with a Latter-day Saint wife with whom they could be sealed in the temple. If Black brothers followed that same pattern, would the same God *not* bless us, based solely on the color of our skin? Aren't the promised blessings predicated upon obedience for *every* member of the Church regardless of race, ethnicity, or Church pioneer ancestry?

> *I have always remembered the feeling of the Spirit when He testified of the truthfulness of the gospel. That burning in my bosom has stayed with me and grounded me in the Church.*

When my time in the US Navy was nearing an end, I sought the next step in my life. I considered going on a mission. I didn't know if it was right for me or what I would be putting myself through. Since I was the only Latter-day Saint in my family and my mother hadn't wanted me to join the Church in the first place, she couldn't understand why and asked, "Why would you even want to serve a mission for a racist church?" Who else was I to talk to but God?

One Sunday afternoon I prayed long and hard, discussing

everything with Him. In the end no inspiration came to answer my prayer. I concluded that a mission wasn't for me and went to sleep. The next day, having had a bad day at work, I decided to walk back to the barracks. I was alone and deep in thought when the word *missionary* came to me in a whisper. I continued walking, and the word came loud this time. MISSIONARY. I was overcome by the Spirit. The burning in my bosom was even stronger than what I had felt when I'd first heard the doctrine of the gospel. I lost track of time while caught up in the Spirit. The next thing I remember was staring at the sun, crying. My answer had come in a way far more powerful than I had wanted. My path was clear in my eyes. I had no doubt that I should serve a mission.

When I entered the Missionary Training Center, I thought I was ready for what was to come, but I wasn't. As one of a small handful of Black missionaries there, I expected to be treated differently and even to be stared at. After all, most of the young people came from all over the world, including places where some had never seen a Black person with their very own eyes. What I wasn't expecting was to be falsely accused of something and for my companion to not just believe it, but to help give it breath. We spent every hour of every day together. We knew each other better than most friends ever know one another. He must have known I was innocent, and the betrayal stung.

Hurt and angered by the accusation, I wanted an apology. It had been reported to the MTC leadership that I had been seen exiting the sisters' dormitory. I was innocent. I was verbally berated and belittled

> *I continued walking, and the word came loud this time.* MISSIONARY. *I was overcome by the Spirit. The burning in my bosom was even stronger than what I had felt when I'd first heard the doctrine of the gospel. . . . My answer had come in a way far more powerful than I had wanted. My path was clear in my eyes. I had no doubt that I should serve a mission.*

for my supposed misconduct and prevented from saying anything to defend myself. Although I was cleared from the false accusation, I received neither an apology nor a public statement of the falsehood. I continued my training in the MTC, and during the remainder of my time there, I encountered stares accompanied by whispers. But I chose to continue my training and mission because I remembered my experience when the Holy Spirit spoke truth to me.

> *I've learned that enduring to the end means treading through the imperfection of others, because none of us are perfect. Others must tread through my imperfections as I tread through theirs, all the while remembering we are all growing and learning step by step.*

Once in the field, I had several White companions who weren't afraid to express their racist views to me, both publicly and privately. I waded through it all, remembering *why* I was there.

In the aftermath of pain caused by racist words or actions of fellow Church members, I've always gone back to the burning in my bosom that I felt when first hearing the doctrine and receiving my spiritual mission call. Those and many more experiences with the Spirit have grounded me in the truth and shielded me against countless racist encounters with members over the years.

I have spent many years reading doctrinal books and talks about the importance of forgiveness. As a Black man in the Church, I've been asked to forgive numerous times when others misunderstood or mistreated me because of the color of my skin. I've been called a pioneer in the Church many times too, which I take as meaning that my struggles might help others overcome theirs. That's why I decided to share and be part of this project: (1) to help my Black brothers and sisters know they're not alone, and (2) to help my White brothers and sisters understand that their continuing to hold on to racist attitudes and actions is preventing unity. Jesus commanded: "I say unto you, be one; and if ye are not one ye are not mine" (Doctrine and Covenants 38:27). Holding on to racist ideologies impedes us from being one. If we are not one (united), then we do not belong to Jesus.

The road to perfection is a long journey. I've learned that enduring to the end means treading through the imperfection of others, because none of us are perfect. Others must tread through my imperfections as I tread through theirs, all the while remembering we are all growing and learning step by step. I'm trying to live my life with this one concept: judge people less and try to understand them more. I cannot change others' racist beliefs; that's between them and the Lord on Judgment Day. Consistently, I am reminded that I'm not a human being on a spiritual journey but a spiritual being on a human journey. Satan wants us to believe that we are alone and isolated in our pain. But Christ walks with us, and the Spirit strengthens us as we allow Christ to take our pain; with Them we are never alone or isolated.

We must push forward, not allowing situations to doubt or abandon our testimonies. We must not allow the actions of some members to dictate our actions toward other members or toward the Church. We must persist in using the principles of the gospel to dictate our actions toward all people, including members of the Church.

> *Satan wants us to believe that we are alone and isolated in our pain. But Christ walks with us, and the Spirit strengthens us as we allow Christ to take our pain; with Them we are never alone or isolated.*

I have met many great and inspiring people in the Church. I have learned that although the color of my skin determines how I'm viewed as a man to many people in this life, it doesn't determine the type of man I am before God. A man's heart and actions are what matters to Him.[3] Although as Black men, we have a history in the US, individually and collectively, of being

---

3. See 1 Samuel 16:7: "For the Lord seeth not as man seeth; for man looketh on the outward appearance, but the Lord looketh on the heart."

mistreated and looked at as lesser than, God sees us with eyes of knowledge from our beginning in His presence to our time here in mortality. In the face of all that has happened and all that will happen, enduring to the end is the most important thing for us to do in this life. It is important to allow Christ to deal with the unrighteousness of this world because each man and woman will stand accountable to Him in the end.

I have learned to stand back up when I've been hurt, to give my pain to Christ, and to not abandon the truth. The road to exaltation is not paved with excuses, but with faith and repentance. The integrity of our testimonies will always be challenged by Satan, but our strength comes from the Spirit of the Lord, uplifting us as He has promised: "But they that wait upon the Lord shall renew their strength; they shall mount up with wings as eagles" (Isaiah 40:31).

WITHOUT*

There it was.
Towering before Us, Your Spiritual Ancestors.
THE TEMPLE OF GOD.
Housed therein was total Truth and Revelation
And the Ordinances for Exaltation.
Ordinances that bound Husband to Wife in Chosen Love.
Ordinances that kept Children with Parents for eternity.
Ordinances that were just for the Children of God.
"Are we too not Children of God?"
We cried looking to Heaven from whence always came our Help.
Some of Us were always Free.
But even Free . . . we understood.
We knew what was done.

And from God's own mouth
To our very ears
We heard and held The Truth
That would have stilled their beings in fright.
The Truth the Trumpet sounded in our souls.

—*Alice Faulkner Burch*

---

* Without: the absence or lack of something or someone; on the outside; an outer place or area.

I THOUGHT THE GOSPEL WAS FREE FOR ANYONE THAT WANTED TO HEAR IT

MARIE BENJAMIN GRAVES
1878–1930

Marie Benjamin Graves worked as a dressmaker. She was married to William Graves (1858–1940) in 1909. Their marriage was officiated by a Latter-day Saint missionary, although they were not members of the Church at the time; they were baptized November 21, 1911. From the beginning of their membership in the Church, both Marie and William participated actively in the Oakland Branch in Oakland, California. Four months after their baptism, both stood to bear their testimonies. From that time forward, one or both bore their testimonies at least every other month. Sometimes Marie requested that the congregation sing the hymn "Guide Us, O Thou Great Jehovah" to help her express her testimony. Marie remained a faithful member of the Church to the die she died at age fifty-two.[1]

I feel that it is right for me to let you know how I was treated when I visited this branch of the Church in Atlanta, Ga. I had some friends I wanted to take to church because I did not know when I would have that opportunity again, so I asked two friends to go with me to church. We found the right church all right, but found the wrong people. It seems like I had gone into a den of evil spirits, so bad was the feelings

---

1. Ardis E. Parshall, "William and Marie Graves: 'We Found the Right Church, All Right . . .'" *Keepapitchinin* (blog), September 30, 2015, http://www.keepapitchinin.org/2018/09/12/william-and-marie-graves-we-found-the-right-church-all-right/; September 14, 2018, http://www.keepapitchinin.org/2018/09/14/marie-and-william-graves-the-part-i-withheld/. Used with permission from Ardis E. Parshall, historical researcher, who holds a copy of the original document used here.

against us because we was Colored.² I told one or two of the members of that branch that I was a member in Oakland, Calif. Two or three tried to make us welcome. I was told that the conference president would come and see me later. I suppose that it was the conference president come to us and said that he wanted to speak to us on the outside, so we went out. He told us of the line being between the Colored and the White people and antagonistic feeling among them and the church being dedicated by the White people of the South. When he finish we said goodbye and left. We knew that meant for us to stay out of there.

We knew the line was drawn in the South. We did not go up in the front. We sit in the back and finally was asked out of the church. I never had nothing to hurt me like that in all of my life.

My friends said now you belong to that church and cannot go to it here. Had I known we would have been treated like that I never would have tried to have gone to church there. I felt so much worse by my friends being with me and seeing how mean they acted. I was very glad one's husband did not get there until we had been put out, and we did not tell him what had happened. We said that we just decided to go to another church. And the other husband did not leave home. We decided not to tell our husbands. We did not need any more company feeling bad with us.

I feel like I have done my duty any way. The blame will not be on me. They don't ask no one out of the other White churches because they are Colored down there. After I was treated like this I could not leave the South fast enough.

I thought the Gospel was free for any one that wanted to hear it. I did not know that it was like that down there. I have a testimony of

---

2. This was written by Ms. Marie in 1920. At that time, "Colored" was what both Black Americans called themselves and what White Americans called us. It is appropriate to the time period. This term is not appropriate to use today.

the Gospel just the same. The Lord has blessed me wonderfully and I thank Him for it.³

> *Guide us, O Thou great Jehovah,*
> *Guide us to the promised land.*
> *We are weak, but Thou art able;*
> *Hold us with Thy pow'rful hand.*
> *Holy Spirit, Holy Spirit,*
> *Feed us till the Savior comes.*
>
> *Open, Jesus, Zion's fountains;*
> *Let her richest blessings come.*
> *Let the fiery, cloudy pillar*
> *Guard us to this holy home.*
> *Great Redeemer, Great Redeemer,*
> *Bring, oh, bring the welcome day.*
>
> *When the earth begins to tremble,*
> *Bid our fearful thoughts be still;*
> *When Thy judgments spread destruction,*
> *Keep us safe on Zion's hill,*
> *Singing praises, Singing praises,*
> *Songs of glory unto Thee.*⁴

---

3. Transcript from Parshall, "William and Marie Graves: 'We Found the Right Church, All Right. . . .'" Spelling has been updated for ease of reading. Regardless of what happened in Georgia, Marie *did* remain faithful to the Lord and a dedicated member of the Church. Historical researcher Ardis E. Parshall found these mentions of Marie in the ward records: "Sis Graves spoke of the Lord's goodness to her, and enjoys the gospel more and more each day"; "Sister Graves . . . bore [her] testimony to the truthfulness of the Gospel and the many blessings which [she] had received." In addition, Marie continued to contribute regularly and generously to the charitable funds of the Relief Society.
4. "Guide Us, O Thou Great Jehovah," *Hymns* (1985), no. 83. Originally published in 1762; included in the first Latter-day Saint hymnbook in 1835. This was a favorite hymn of Marie and is shared here as part of her personal testimony, which she often did.

IDENTITY AND PRIORITY

PARKER M. JOLLEY

Parker Jolley graduated high school in Utah in 2020 during the COVID-19 pandemic. He started his service mission in October 2020 in Salt Lake City. His grandfather is his best friend and hero. The fifth child of eight children, he is excited for his future and to see where his path goes as he follows God's plan for him.

In my journey to prepare for and serve a mission, I have learned to honor my identity as both a Black man and a child of God. I faced many struggles, but through faith, strength, and prayer from others and myself, I realize that the Holy Ghost and the Savior are always by my side.

In high school I was constantly surrounded by people who I thought were there to help me and stand by my side but ended up guiding me down the wrong paths. Then the COVID-19 pandemic happened in 2020; in-person seminary was canceled, as was graduation. Protests were being held around Utah and the world, and people were taking sides and stands against injustices done to Black men. I felt like it was getting harder for me to stay on the strait and narrow path. I was constantly being tempted and crippled by the works of Satan. I felt the pressures of trying to stay on the path of God. I felt the pressure of trying to succeed but then failing.

> *I faced many struggles, but through faith, strength, and prayer from others and myself, I realize that the Holy Ghost and the Savior are always by my side.*

IDENTITY AND PRIORITY

I had wanted to be a missionary since I was a child. I focused on preparing, but it was hard for me to navigate the path of becoming a missionary. There were trials every day. During the trials of 2020, my family and I attended protests during the summer. It was hard to see people of my own race fighting against harmful injustice and feeling like I too needed to do something. I felt like it was my duty to speak out against biased judgments and to protest as well. I felt guilty because I wasn't taking action, because I wasn't doing anything to help stand and speak up.

I was confused and distraught, as I was navigating through life without prayer and testimony at the time. Because of all the difficulties taking place and the violence being done to those who look like me, I felt in the wrong mentally and physically. I wanted to understand the pain and agony inflicted upon us for being Black, but all I could find were questions that kept eating away at me. It wasn't easy to ask for help and to pray to the Lord, asking for guidance and seeking to know the answer, when I couldn't even figure out or understand what it was that I was wanting to see.

For quite some time, every first Sunday of each month my family and I attended a Church support group called Genesis in addition to our regular ward. Genesis was like attending a Black church but with all the Latter-day Saint teachings and beliefs. There we would sing, praise the Lord, listen to guest speakers, and hear the choir sing songs that uplifted the soul. Genesis was a place where I felt welcomed. A place where I was able to connect with others of my race, so I never felt out of place. I was able to learn not just of my culture but of the Lord as well. By continuing to attend Genesis, I began feeling the

> *I was able to learn not just of my culture but of the Lord as well. By continuing to attend Genesis, I began feeling the acceptance of others of my race who worshipped the Lord, and I also felt welcomed into a community I was unfamiliar with but where I still belonged.*

acceptance of others of my race who worshipped the Lord, and I also felt welcomed into a community I was unfamiliar with but where I still belonged. But in 2020 during the pandemic, even Genesis was gone, as was the feeling of belonging to a community.

For as long as I can remember I had dreamed of serving a mission in New Zealand, just like my father had done. When I was a young boy, I wanted to be a missionary. I wanted to serve the Lord. I would think of the time when my mother had given me a missionary tag with "Parker Merlyn Jolley, Missionary of the LDS Church" written on it. I would wear that missionary tag every day and everywhere I went. I would teach others what I had learned from church. I wanted to learn more about the Savior and His teachings. I felt very triumphant at that time and was grateful to serve the Lord in as many ways as I could, even though I was a child. I knew that I was a child of God, and that meant I had potential and was important. Years later I didn't feel any of that. I was working so hard just to try to be on the right path.

One of my worries about serving a mission was my disabilities. I tried hard to focus more on my abilities through serving, but I struggled as I proceeded through the mission application process. After feeling agitated while awaiting the arrival of my mission call from our Prophet, President Russell M. Nelson, I was finally given my letter and calling. The calling was a local service mission. Now I was more confused and concerned. I continued to challenge, question, and ask myself, "Why a service mission? Why had the Lord decided I needed to do a service mission?" I wanted to understand. I was challenged with that question every day. I became angry and anxious with myself. I thought I wouldn't be able to fully serve the Lord on a service mission. I felt as though I wasn't able to receive the full experience of a mission, let alone spread the word of the gospel.

I prayed and asked for the reason. After a while my prayer was answered. I began to understand that a proselyting mission isn't the only way to serve the Lord and that He had different ideas for using my special abilities in His work.

One of my favorite scriptures in the Bible says: "Neither do men light a candle, and put it under a bushel, but on a candlestick; and it giveth light unto all that are in the house. Let your light so shine before men, that they may see your good works, and glorify your Father which is in heaven" (Matthew 5:15–16).

Those words hold meaning for me—I am part of God's great work. Fulfilling this service mission as a young Black man is part of His grand design. My service mission is part of His great work.

> *I would wear that missionary tag every day and everywhere I went. I would teach others what I had learned from church. I wanted to learn more about the Savior and His teachings. I felt very triumphant at that time and was grateful to serve the Lord in as many ways as I could, even though I was a child. I knew that I was a child of God, and that meant I had potential and was important.*

Through this work, He designed for me to find the strength I needed to serve and help others. And through this mission, my light will shine before men, they will see the good works I do because I love God, and that will glorify my Heavenly Father.

This is what brought me back into the light:

(1) Attending the protests during the summer of 2020 opened my eyes and heart as I saw so many people of different ethnicities and backgrounds that God created come together to show their support for people who look like me. And for me!

(2) Being constantly on my knees, pleading with God to give me strength.

(3) Fasting every other week, asking for confidence in myself and to know and feel my self-worth.

(4) Serving my family and neighbors.

(5) Reading the scriptures every day.

As a result of my work, effort, and sincerity, I felt God at my side. He became my best friend in the most difficult time of my life.

As I returned into the light, I could see my purpose and the wisdom in being assigned a service mission. As I began to serve, I realized I was given the opportunity to serve the Lord in many different ways, and I was able to stay close to home. President Russell M. Nelson once said, "Be patient with yourself. Perfection comes not in this life, but in the next life. Don't demand things that are unreasonable, but demand of yourself improvement. As you let the Lord help you through that, He will make the difference."[1] I began to recall those words as I started to bring into context that I was finally being given the opportunity to serve Heavenly Father.

I am part of God's great work. Fulfilling this service mission as a young Black man is part of His grand design. My service mission is part of His great work. Through this work, He designed for me to find the strength I needed to serve and help others. And through this mission, my light will shine before men, they will see the good works I do because I love God, and that will glorify my Heavenly Father.

When I was first given the opportunity to serve a mission, I wanted to serve abroad, but the Lord had a different path for me. The Lord was slowly guiding me toward the answers I had been seeking since I was a young child. The Lord continued to guide me through preparing for my mission and serving my mission as well. I was blessed to be able to serve, as my father had done, when I was a little kid with the fake missionary tag. I succeeded in that mission. Then I was blessed to serve another full-time mission as a service missionary. President Nelson said: "In coming days, it will not be possible to survive spiritually without the guiding, directing, comforting,

---

1. Russell M. Nelson, "Men's Hearts Shall Fail Them" (video), https://www.churchofjesuschrist.org/study/video/inspirational-messages/2011-11-020-mens-hearts-shall-fail-them?lang=eng.

IDENTITY AND PRIORITY

and constant influence of the Holy Ghost."[2] Without Heavenly Father sending the Holy Ghost to guide me through the trials I had, I wouldn't have been able to continue.

There have been many trials and errors in serving the Lord and spreading the gospel as an African American man. Many people I have encountered weren't easily trusting or didn't want to learn because of who they perceived me to be. I was looked upon as a Black man and a Black man only. It was hard for me because I felt I was getting nowhere. As a young Black man serving the Lord, I felt like I was constantly being pressured to be a role model to others while protests were happening. At the same time, I was looked upon as being different and unalike to many. It tested my confidence in myself and also my testimony, since I was required and guided to find my own strength during those trying times. I also asked for help when I was directed and needed to.

I am thankful for all of the opportunities, blessings, and help I have been given. This is the path Heavenly Father has given to me, and I will continue to follow that path each and every day, hopefully helping others on the way. I am thankful enough to have been brought back to the light, to oppose the works of Satan, and to focus on what Heavenly Father had guided me to do. Through prayer, I am able to focus on serving the Lord and Savior as an African American Latter-day Saint missionary. As I've learned to honor my identity as a Black man and a child of God and learned proper priority in my life, I know for myself that these words said by President Nelson are true: "Your life will be a blessed and balanced experience if you first honor your identity and priority."[3]

---

2. Russell M. Nelson, "Revelation for the Church, Revelation for Our Lives," *Ensign*, May 2018.
3. Russell M. Nelson, "Identity, Priority, and Blessings," *Ensign*, August 2001.

THE FAMILY WITH THE BLACK KIDS

ABIGAIL HANSEN

Abigail Hansen works as a paraprofessional at a school for children with various learning disabilities, where her students know her as "Ms. Abi." She loves absolutely every minute of being with her sweet students. Abigail currently lives in Provo, Utah, completing her education to become a special education teacher. She is a dancer and loves the holidays.

I'm a twenty-one-year-old Black woman living in the Latter-day Saint bubble of Utah and Idaho. My experience is not like those around me. Due to the difficult circumstances of my birth family, I was put up for adoption and raised by a White family on a farm in Idaho Falls. I had a great childhood within the walls of my home. My family was very supportive, especially of my interests.

Though my family was supportive, it wasn't always so great being the only family with Black children in our ward. Fortunately, I had two brothers who were also Black. Sometimes when we would attend stake activities, we would see another Black kid. After being in a sea of White people all the time, honestly, the highlight of my week was the comfort of knowing that I wasn't alone. The way my family was sometimes treated openly at church bothered me. We were always described as "the family with the Black kids," or something along those lines—"the Black kids" was always the main identifier. Why not "the family with nine kids" or "the family that lives on a farm"? There were more options, but I felt people didn't even try to go beyond using a description that cast us three kids as being "other."

Socially it has been difficult being Black in an area where the Church is dominated by White culture. People would touch my hair without asking, and then they would say it was greasy. At girls' camp other young people would get some sun and say, "Look! I'm almost as dark as you, Abi!" I was always being compared to things that were dark or black. I hated whenever the topic of Black people and the priesthood came up. The other kids would break their necks just to see what my reaction was. I always stayed quiet to hear what these folks had to say about something that they claimed no longer mattered because it was so long ago; they would tell me and other Black people to "move on" when we talked about racism and slavery. I refused to be the spokesperson for my entire race or to be told why I and my ancestors deserved to be punished for our skin color.

After being in a sea of White people all the time, honestly, the highlight of my week was the comfort of knowing that I wasn't alone.

The biggest social stigma in the Church as a teenager was about dating people like me. I've always remembered what I heard once in a movie. The father of a young woman told her very calmly: "These White men are dangerous." By the time I was a teenager, I knew if I was not careful, the words and actions of some White people in my ward would be detrimental to my self-esteem and my self-view as being divine. I was never asked to dance or asked on a date. It was always hurtful to see the White girls and boys in my graduating seminary class ask each other out all the time, while I was not just ignored but treated as though I was invisible or didn't exist. There were definitely times I felt unwanted and undesirable. After all, what did these other teenagers have that I didn't?

As I've grown into young adulthood, I have slowly realized that some of the guys viewed Black women as scary and not an acceptable person they could take home to their moms. Well, I didn't want to date those kinds of people anyway.

Many of those around me haven't been at all worried about my feelings. I've even been told that I just wasn't White *enough*. I've felt as though others were trying to change me to fit some kind of mold or idea that they had in their head of what I should be or how I should look. I was free-spirited and would color my hair a million different shades, and as a result I was told that I wasn't temple worthy and would not raise temple-worthy children. (For the record, Black women are dope and can raise some even more dope children in the gospel.)

The part that has been the most difficult for me to reconcile has been that while I always felt special and loved growing up, when I turned nineteen and went to college at BYU–Idaho, all of that changed.

When so many Black men died during 2020 from being detained by the police and others, my heart hurt. I wasn't able to escape it. People talked about it. People posted about it on social media. The way my extended family, some Church leaders, and people I grew up with talked about Black people hurt too. I would lie in my room and cry until I couldn't cry anymore. It was as if they had forgotten that people like me were seeing these events. Then when I defended the person being hurt or killed, I was told, "I love you, Abi, but . . ." and "This is just how it is." I haven't been able to look at those people the same since.

> *I think it speaks to the power of the testifying Spirit and the enduring truth of the gospel that I and other Black people stay in the Church despite often being made to feel we are less than.*

I learned that year that these people who I thought loved me and were my friends were not safe for me to be around. That realization still hurts. Sometimes it's still like a fresh wound. It seemed like people were saying, "Love one another *as long as* . . ." with all these rules and conditions added.

THE FAMILY WITH THE BLACK KIDS

Something I often say is, "I love the Church and I love the gospel, but sometimes I hate Church members." If it weren't for my knowledge and my testimony, I wouldn't be in the Church, quite honestly. I don't blame those Black men and women that leave the Church. Is that sad? Yes. But there are many ways it can be traumatic to be a Black member. But I think it speaks to the power of the testifying Spirit and the enduring truth of the gospel that I and other Black people stay in the Church despite often being made to feel we are less than.

> *I love God. He has been there for me during my highest of highs and lowest of lows. He loves me unconditionally. He is aware of me.*

I love God. He has been there for me during my highest of highs and lowest of lows. He loves me unconditionally. He is aware of me. Very aware of me: Abigail Hansen. I know He is proud of me. Because of this, because I know, I am still in the Church.

JESUS UNDERSTANDS ME BLACK

Jesus understands me Black
Jesus understands me.

When the Leaders who promised
to watch-over look past me,
Jesus understands me Black
because He had to chastise Leaders
for scattering the Sheep they were
appointed to gather in.

When I am accused of theft
or lying or being too high falsely
Jesus understands me Black
because Falsifiers crucified Him
because Accusers said He committed
blasphemy when He is the Son of the Almighty.

When those who said they were my
friends and had my back walked away
leaving me unprotected in the hurricane,
Jesus understood me Black
because a brother who spoke commitment and loyalty
gave Him to the tormentors with a kiss.

When my knees are marked from kneeling long
and my body ached from sleepless prayer-filled nights
begging for protection or help or deliverance,
Jesus understands me Black
because in Gethsemane every pore opened
to spill understanding compassionate blood
and on a hill called Calvary were His hands marked
not once but twice in
witness of Him as Son Who Gave
for all like me who kneel
and upon us He puts the title of
"My Own," "My Child," "My Daughter," "My Son."

Jesus understands me Black
Jesus understands me.

—*Alice Faulkner Burch*

IS THAT STILL A THING?

ROBERT S. BURCH JR.

Robert S. Burch Jr. was born in Atlanta, Georgia, and attended Talladega College. He is a member of Omega Psi Phi Fraternity, one of the first all-Black fraternities. He has been a member of the Church for thirty-five years. Robert is founder and executive director of the Sema Hadithi African American Heritage and Culture Foundation, an organization founded in Utah focused solely on Black history. He resides with his wife, Alice, in Utah.

Is Black discomfort still a thing?

Is Black anger still a thing?

Is Black paranoia *still* a thing?[1]

Is Black distrust of White people still a thing? Even if they are members of The Church of Jesus Christ of Latter-day Saints?

Is that still a thing?

Unequivocally it is.

---

1. Black paranoia has been described as "fears and suspicions about hidden forms for race-based animus. . . . We can counteract racial paranoia in the twenty-first century by taking its pessimism seriously and admitting the duplicities that sometimes define inter-racial dialogues" (John L. Jackson Jr., *Racial Paranoia: The Unintended Consequences of Political Correctness* [Civitas Books, 2008]). Other researchers note, "Recent theoretical models suggest that perceived racism acts as a stressor for African Americans and may be associated with a variety of negative psychological consequences, notably paranoia. . . . This study examined the relationship between perceived racism and paranoia" and found that "perceived racism predicted cultural mistrust" (Dennis R. Combs and others, "Perceived Racism as a Predictor among African Americans," *Journal of Black Psychology*, February 1, 2006, https://doi.org/10.1177/0095798405283175). Similarly, the term *racial battle fatigue*, coined by University of Utah professor William A. Smith, PhD, describes this phenomenon as the symptoms that Black people and people of color develop due to the burden of a lifetime of racism.

And as long as it is a thing, I remain faith-filled that the gospel of Jesus Christ is the only way to uplift and obtain salvation in our earthly struggle. It succors in the depths of virulent hatred, after we have done all that we can do.

For the four hundred years Black Christians have lived on the North American continent, we have been marginalized and slowly robbed of our rights and freedoms. In the face of betrayal from our White brethren, Black Christians have only one sure friend to call on: Jesus Christ. Uncertain of which of our earthly siblings we can be sure of, Christ has never left a doubt that we can count on Him and that He has our back.[2]

> *To not remain a Latter-day Saint or Christian is to walk away from that which has been ours from the beginning.*

Despite the betrayal and racism, why are African Americans still members of the Church? Why are we even still Christian? The answer, in part, is that to not remain a Latter-day Saint or Christian is to walk away from that which has been ours from the beginning.

In 1619, the first Angolans to disembark as captives from a ship in colonial Virginia were Christian.[3] They came from a part of the world that was Christian seventy years before Spain, Portugal, or England.[4] A few in Spain would adopt Arianism (a form of Christianity) around

---

2. See Doctrine and Covenants 49:27: "Behold, I will go before you and be your rearward; and I will be in your midst, and you shall not be confounded." See also Doctrine and Covenants 84:88; Isaiah 52:12; 3 Nephi 21:29.
3. "Meet the 20 and Odd and Hear Their Story," video, Ric Murphy, Federation of Genealogical Societies Annual Conference, August 21–24, 2019, https://www.facebook.com/aahgs/videos/390470904943259/.
4. "Christianity - Aksum embraced the Orthodox tradition of Christianity in the 4th century (c. 340–356 C.E.) under the rule of King Ezana. The king had been converted by Frumentius, a former Syrian captive who was made Bishop of Aksum." "The Kingdom of Aksum," Trustees of the British Museum, accessed August 30, 2021, https://www.khanacademy.org/humanities/art-africa/east-africa2/ethiopia/a/the-kingdom-of-aksum.

AD 360,[5] but Christianity would not become a predominant religion until 410. For 711 years, from 781 to 1492, the area of Hispania (the Iberian Peninsula, Spain, and Portugal) would evolve through many dispensations of expansion before becoming Christian nations.[6] For more than one thousand years after Christ, Christianity struggled to gain a foothold in England, from the mission of Augustine in AD 597 to the Norman Conquest ending in 1075.[7] Before any of those events, Aksum (Ethiopia) became the first Christian nation in AD 340.[8]

> *I remain faith-filled that the gospel of Jesus Christ is the only way to uplift and obtain salvation in our earthly struggle. It succors in the depths of virulent hatred, after we have done all that we can do.*

Much of the collection of revelation we call scripture today comes from the region of the Mediterranean surrounding North Africa and Persia. We recognize these places today as Tunisia, Libya, Egypt, Sudan, Saudi Arabia, Israel, Jordan, Lebanon, Syria, Iraq, and Turkey.

The language of hatred so often used today is not born in a void. It is born out of more than seven hundred years of military, political, and religious dominance over Africans. By the middle of the 1400s, the language of hatred toward Africans was well developed, as witnessed by the words of Gomes Zurara in his journal: "The seamen began to

---

5. Arianism receives its name from the presbyter, ascetic, and priest Arius who was from the coast of what is now Libya in Africa. See Kaufmann Kohler and Samuel Krauss, "Arianism," JewishEncyclopedia.com, accessed August 30, 2021, https://web.archive.org/web/20120110155839/http://www.jewishencyclopedia.com/articles/1757-arianism.
6. See Stanley Payne, *Spanish Catholicism: An Historical Overview* (Madison, WI: University of Wisconsin Press, 1984), 3–11.
7. See "Saint Augustine of Canterbury," Franciscan Media, accessed August 30, 2021, https://www.franciscanmedia.org/saint-of-the-day/saint-augustine-of-canterbury; "The Church in Norman England," Schoolshistory.org.uk, accessed August 30, 2021, https://schoolshistory.org.uk/topics/church-norman-england/.
8. See Linda M. Heywood, "Slavery and Its Transformation in the Kingdom of Kongo: 1491–1800," *The Journal of African History* 50, no. 1 (2009): 1–22.

make ready their boats, and to take out those captives, and carry them on shore, as they were commanded. And these, placed all together in that field,

> *Christ has never left a doubt that we can count on Him and that He has our back.*

were a marvellous sight; for amongst them were some white enough, fair to look upon, and well proportioned; others were less white like mulattoes; others again were as black as Ethiops, and so ugly, both in features and in body, as almost to appear (to those who saw them) the images of a lower hemisphere."[9] The Christian faith soon adopted this language of intellectual and scientific contempt.

Through several papal bulls, the Catholic Church penned declarations that fully demonstrate the adoption of anti-African language.[10] The Church of Jesus Christ of Latter-day Saints claims to have thrown off racist apostate teachings. However, many of its members have fostered long-held beliefs and used anti-African Diaspora[11] rhetoric.[12] The perception that some of these beliefs are canonized truths continues to create divisions among modern-day Latter-day Saints.

Then why stay a member of the Church? Why stay Christian?

---

9. Gomes Eannes de Azurara, *The Chronicle of the Discovery and Conquest of Guinea*, vol. 1 (London: Hakluyt Society, 1896), 31, 81.
10. Papal bulls are public decrees issued by the pope of the Catholic Church. See also "Romanus Pontifex (Granting the Portuguese a Perpetual Monopoly in Trade with Africa), January 8, 1455," Papal Encyclicals Online, accessed August 30, 2021, https://www.papalencyclicals.net/nichol05/romanus-pontifex.htm.
11. Diaspora: 2 a: people settled far from their ancestral homelands; members of the African Diaspora; b: the place where these people live; c: the movement, migration, or scattering of a people away from an established or ancestral home land. (Merriam-Webster online dictionary, https://www.merriam-webster.com/dictionary/diaspora)
12. See Lester E. Bush Jr., "Mormonism's Negro Doctrine: An Historical Overview," *Dialogue: A Journal of Mormon Thought* 34, nos. 1/2 (Spring/Summer 2001): 225–93. For example, in Brigham Young's 1852 address to Utah, he stated, "The seed of Canaan will inevitably carry the curse which was placed upon them, until the same authority which placed it there, shall see proper to re-move it." *Journal of Discourses*, 7:290–91 (October 9, 1859).

Since the time of Jesus, people of African descent have been His disciples. The gospel He learned and taught was lived by Africans and Persians thousands of years before Jesus was actualized in the flesh. Christianity has been ours from the beginning. It is a daily frustration to deal with those who would make us less than children of God after we have adopted the beliefs of our people. Their tradition of hatred separates Black people from success, safety, health, common charity, and peace of mind.

Is that still a thing?

Yes! It is still a thing.

Yet because of the succor and the salvation the gospel offers, I remain faithful. I remain confident in the plans and works of God. I look to the counsel of the righteous whom God ordains to help the congregation of the believing mature in His word, understanding that every individual is ultimately responsible for the work of their own salvation, not those family, friends, or even Church leaders who might err, lie, or be confounded in their words. It is imperative to continue the work of building the universal kingdom of God by righteous means, individually and collectively, in the unity of truth.

> *If a White person hates a Black person and then that Black person hates the White person because they first hated them, the only one who wins is Lucifer. . . . As children of God, we cannot answer hate with hate.*

As has always been done in the African American community, we must remain steadfast in Christ. A knowledge of the scriptures, the companionship of the Holy Spirit, a sure witness of Jesus the Christ—as personified by service to others—these are how we best become more godlike in our fellowship to others. I understand that if a White person hates a Black person and then that Black person hates the White person because they first hated them, the only one who wins is Lucifer, the trickster, because both are deceived. As children of God, we cannot answer hate with hate, nor a lie with a lie.

God lives. Jesus is the Christ. The prophets of God are found in The Church of Jesus Christ of Latter-day Saints. The ultimate saving and exalting ordinances are taught in the congregation of the believing in meetinghouses and temples throughout the world. And after all we can do, we are saved by Christ's sacrifice and God's grace in judgment.[13]

---

13. See 2 Nephi 25:23: "For we labor diligently to write, to persuade our children, and also our brethren, to believe in Christ, and to be reconciled to God; for we know that it is by grace that we are saved, after all we can do." See also 2 Nephi 10:24; 2 Nephi 31:20–21; Romans 4; Ephesians 2:8–9; 2 Timothy 1:9; Bible Dictionary, "Grace."

"THE TRUMPET SOUNDS WITHIN MY SOUL"

TESTIMONIES OF TRUTH

"I would like to bear my testimony to you. I know this is the true church. I know Joseph Smith is a true prophet of God that he translated the Book of Mormon. I know Spencer W. Kimball is a prophet of God. I know God lives, that Jesus Christ is our Savior & Redeemer. These things I say in the name of Jesus Christ. Amen."

—Freda Lucretia Magee Beaulieu
1899–1991; baptized June 28, 1909

NOTHING SMALL IN THE KINGDOM OF GOD

SAMUEL DAVIDSON CHAMBERS
1831–1929

Samuel Davidson Chambers was born enslaved in Pickens County, Alabama, in 1831 to Hester Gillespie, an enslaved woman, and James Davidson, their enslaver. In 1844, at approximately thirteen years old, he accepted the gospel and was baptized. For a quarter of a century he had no further contact with the Church and no hope of ever joining the body of the Saints. Unable to read or write and lacking parents or peers or missionaries to encourage him in his youthful faith, he retained his testimony solely through the Holy Spirit. Without missionary encouragement or assistance from the Perpetual Emigration Fund, Samuel brought his family to Utah in 1870. On May 1, 1873, Samuel was appointed as assistant deacon but did not receive the priesthood. In January 1876, he received a vote of thanks for his faithful discharge of these duties. With his wife, Amanda, they received wide recognition for the quality of their produce, especially their grapes and currants, and were awarded first prize in several agricultural fairs. The Chamberses were consistent tithe payers all their lives.[1]

---

1. "Saint without Priesthood: The Collected Testimonies of Ex-Slave Samuel D. Chambers," *Dialogue: A Journal of Mormon Thought* 12 (Summer 1979): 13–21, used with permission; Ronald Coleman, "Samuel D. Chambers (1831–1929) and Amanda Chambers (1840–1925)," Black Past, October 25, 2016, https://www.blackpast.org/african-american-history/people-african-american-history/chambers-samuel-d-1831-1929-and-amanda-chambers-1840-1925/. See also Coleman, R. (2016, October 25). Samuel D. Chambers (1831–1929) and Amanda Chambers (1840–1925). BlackPast.org. https://www.blackpast.org/african-american-history/people-african-american-history/chambers-samuel-d-1831-1929-and-amanda-chambers-1840-1925/.

May 6, 1873[2]

[I know] the Church is true. . . . [I] knew it from the time the Elders laid their hands on [me]. [I feel] to be active in doing what [I] can do for the building up of the kingdom of God. . . . [I feel] glad to have the privilege to pay tithing and donations.

June 3, 1873

It is a joy . . . to fill all calls made upon [me]. . . . [B]een 29 years in the Church, [I feel] as youthful as ever. . . . When [I have] lived up to the law of tithing, [I have] never lacked anything. May God help us to be faithful.

July 1, 1873

It is good for us to meet together, and speak to each other.

August 5, 1873

I love to meet with Saints, no matter what meeting, it does me good. . . . As I have been appointed a deacon I feel to fulfill my mission. I feel happy to meet any of my brethren. I hope I may always be valiant. May God help me as I grow older in days, that I may ever live with the saints, in time and in eternity.

October 14, 1873

I feel least among the servants of God. I know it is the work of God, but I did not come to Utah to find it out. I ask an interest in your faith and prayers that I may prove faithful to the end.

November 11, 1873

Notwithstanding all my weakness and failings, I feel to fulfill every calling, and desire to attend to every duty when called, and bear

---

2. The following transcript is a selection of individual testimonies from Samuel, which were recorded 1873–1877 by the ward clerk Thomas C. Jones. The transcript comes from "Saint Without Priesthood: The Collected Testimonies of Ex-Slave Samuel D. Chambers," *Dialogue: A Journal of Mormon Thought*, Vol. 12, Summer 1979, pages 13–21. Used by permission.

my testimony. I have a source of satisfaction in meeting with the saints. Tho' a small company yet as the Saviour said "Where two or three are met together in my name I will be in the midst to bless them."[3] I hope it may be the case to-night. I know we are the people of God. We have been led to these peaceful vallies of the mountains, and we enjoy life and a many other blessings. I don't get tired of being with the Latter-day Saints, nor of being one of them. I'm glad that I ever took upon me the name of Christ. It is our privilege to call our families together, and we can sleep sweetly, and rise and thank God in the morning for his care thro' the night. It is good when we can go about our business, and return again, and find all right. I've a good woman and that is a great blessing.[4] I thank God, for my soul burns with love for the many blessings I enjoy. I've been blest from my youth up, altho in bondage for 20 years after receiving the gospel, yet I kept the faith. I thank God that I ever gathered with the Saints. May the Lord bless us and help us to be faithful is my prayer.

> *I feel to fulfill every calling, and desire to attend to every duty when called, and bear my testimony. I have a source of satisfaction in meeting with the saints.*

December 9, 1873

I feel strong in the gospel. I never feel encouraged to fall back but to do my duty. I thank God for all his blessings. I enjoy the good instructions given to us. May we go on, and fulfill our duty as a people is my prayer.

---

3. Matthew 18:20: "For where two or three are gathered together in my name, there am I in the midst of them."
4. Amanda Leggroan Chambers (January 1, 1840–March 10, 1929) was a faithful and dedicated member of the Church to the day she passed. Although there are Relief Society notes that she often bore her testimony, nothing as yet has been found in her own words. During the time when sisters paid dues to be a member of the Relief Society, Amanda was a member, and it is noted that she paid her membership dues.

February 10, 1874

The oftener I bear testimony the better I feel, it strengthens me.

May 12, 1874

It is a source of satisfaction to me to feel that I have the Kingdom of God at heart. I have been a member of this Church a many years, yet it seems but a few days. I was baptized in the year 1844 and after that I was 21 years in bondage, during which time I never heard a word of the gospel. The spirit of God remained within me. In 1865 I was liberated. I then commenced to save means to gather. This took me 4 years. I have rejoiced in the blessings of God thro' all my life. Tho' lacking age and experience yet God kept the seeds of life alive within me. I feel to be as clay in the hands of the potter. I don't boast in my own strength. I ask an interest in your prayers to help me to be faithful. I have joy in cleaning up and whatever I am called to do. I have my weaknesses in connection with all men. I pray that we may be as one to build up the Kingdom of God.

> *The knowledge I received is from my God. It is a high and holy calling, without the testimony of God we are nothing. I pray God that we may live true and faithful to the end.*

August 11, 1874

I know this is the church and kingdom of God. I know it is my duty to bear testimony as well as my privilege. I feel timid, yet I ought not, because I know it is my duty to be obedient. I may rebel once, but I pray God to help me to keep the prize in view. I desire to live my religion, so that I can rise and say I know the gospel I embraced in my youth is true. This causes me to tell the truth. I ask an interest in your faith and prayers that I may live obedient to those set over us. I feel to step forward and vote, and done it with all my power, and gave it all to my friends. I feel proud I've done it. I looked, and can't see when or where I've done wrong to any of the servants of God.

December 8, 1874

There is a call for us all, those of us who came here as well as those who were born here. We have met to exchange our views and ideas, as to our everyday duties. I have a great relish for the work I am engaged in. I realize it is all in the gospel. I was not so well placed as these young brethren here, most of you were born in the church. I was born in a condition of slavery, and received the gospel in that condition. I realized I had done right. I received the spirit of God. I was only between 12 and 13 years of age. . . . The knowledge I received is from my God. It is a high and holy calling, without the testimony of God we are nothing. I pray God that we may live true and faithful to the end.

January 13, 1875

I testify that the gospel is true. I have done so many a time in my youth. I feel blest. I feel to press forward. I feel to say "God bless the Faithful."

September 14, 1875

I'm pleased I live in this day and age when God has spoken from the heavens. I know the brethren who teach us are men of God and if we will put away our weaknesses we shall grow, and I pray that we may ever continue.

October 12, 1875

I know the gospel is true. I received this knowledge in the country where the gospel came to me. I desire to have your faith and prayers, that I may prove faithful, for I realize I shall not have any reward unless I endure to the end. It is there where those who run well will get their reward. May God help us to be faithful is my prayer and desire.

December 14, 1875

I hope we may prove by our works we are determined to carry out the will of God. I'm pleased the Almighty has seen fit to call forth his holy priesthood. He has said you shall hear my voice, for I will declare it by my servants. May the Lord be with us. I realize it is the work of God. I did not come here to find it out, but went forth, not having kind parents as you have, but heard for myself between 10 and 12 years of age. We should be awake. It is a great privilege to us all to be permitted to speak. Joseph was a boy and also Samuel, and the Lord spoke to them, so we see the Lord is willing to speak to boys.

January 12, 1876

It seems to be my privilege to bear my testimony. We are blest with this privilege from time to time. I esteem it the more, the older I get. I am numbered in the quorum, with you, and if I don't bear my testimony, how do you know how I feel, or how you feel? But if I rise and speak, I know I have a friend, and if I hear you speak as I speak, I know we are one. I pray God to bless those who preside over us in this quorum for where they speak to us, it is the same as the word of God. May we be permitted to live on the earth, and do good to each other, is my prayer.

June 12, 1876

Some think it is small to be a deacon. . . . I think there is nothing small in the kingdom of God. David said "I'd rather be a doorkeeper in the house of my God than to dwell in the tents of wickedness."[5]

August 14, 1876

I feel there is much to come to pass and it will come shortly. . . . It has been said that "God and one good man are a great majority."[6] I

---

5. Psalm 84:10: "For a day in thy courts is better than a thousand. I had rather be a doorkeeper in the house of my God, than to dwell in the tents of wickedness."
6. Origin of quote unknown; potentially a paraphrase from Frederick Douglass (February 14, 1818–February 20, 1895), who purportedly said: "*One* and *God* make a *majority*" (https://www.brainyquote.com/quotes/frederick_douglass _105354), and "The man who is right is a majority. He who has God and conscience on his side, has a majority against the universe" (https://www.goodreads .com/quotes/537059-the-man-who-is-right-is-a-majority-he-who).

never regretted doing anything to build up the Kingdom of God. I'm pleased to live in this day and age "when the Lord has set his hand again, a second time to recover a remnant of his people."[7] We are on a sure footing and we will live and if we live our religion we shall enjoy the Spirit of it. I never feel better than while I'm engaged in my duty.

September 11, 1876

I pray to God to help us to do His will, that we may be exalted in His kingdom, is my prayer in the name of Jesus.

November 13, 1876

I could not see (for a while) how I could pay tithing and live. But the spirit said to me, "All things are possible with God."[8] I never questioned it any longer. May the spirit of God be with us that we may never doubt. I feel thankful to be one with you. I pray God to bless you.

> *If I don't bear my testimony, how do you know how I feel, or how you feel? But if I rise and speak, I know I have a friend, and if I hear you speak as I speak, I know we are one.*

---

7. Isaiah 11:11–12: "And it shall come to pass in that day, that the Lord shall set his hand again the second time to recover the remnant of his people, which shall be left, from Assyria, and from Egypt, and from Pathros, and from Cush, and from Elam, and from Shinar, and from Hamath, and from the islands of the sea. And he shall set up an ensign for the nations, and shall assemble the outcasts of Israel, and gather together the dispersed of Judah from the four corners of the earth."
8. Matthew 19:26: "But Jesus beheld them, and said unto them, With men this is impossible; but with God all things are possible."

LEARNING THE GOSPEL AS A YOUNG WOMAN

TIANNA JOLLEY

Tianna Jolley is fourteen years old and lives in Utah. She and her eight siblings are all adopted. She is in middle school and plays the violin and piano. Tianna also currently plays volleyball and basketball as a hobby but soon hopes to try out for varsity teams. She loves reading literature and poetry, especially from Edgar Allen Poe, Mark Twain, Harper Lee, and William Faulkner.

I remember the first time I realized that I had a testimony of the gospel of Jesus Christ. It was an astonishing revelation that I felt in my whole being. I knew then that through testimony I would be strengthened in my faith and in my principles as a young woman of God. When I finally turned the required age to join Young Women, I remember feeling like I had a duty to serve God. I was so excited and hope-filled. I felt that I had a responsibility to exercise my knowledge of the gospel and to learn of Christ's works and miracles that He had given to us, His young daughters—an assignment for us to help carry His message forth.

As I started to envelop myself in the process of serving the Lord, hardships and trials came my way and questions and doubts of the gospel arose in me. But I wanted to learn and to understand. So every other Sunday, when my Young Women leaders would present part of the "Young Women Theme" and challenge us to apply it in our daily lives, I took those assignments seriously. But the harder I worked to do this and to learn the principles better, the harder it was for me to believe in my own divine nature and eternal destiny.

LEARNING THE GOSPEL AS A YOUNG WOMAN

As I participated in various school and Church activities and attended to all my school duties while striving to live the gospel, I struggled to continuously and consistently establish my faith. Divine nature. Eternal destiny. Daughter of God. Disciple of Jesus Christ. I didn't feel a connection with these words. I was able to say the words, but as they left my mouth, they were disconnected from my thoughts and seemed only part of a routine. I didn't know how to connect them *to* me.

I continually asked myself questions: Why am I struggling when I know I can always turn to Christ? Why can't I find the answers I'm searching for promptly instead of wanting to turn to the Church leaders for help? Would Christ always be there to support me? Would the Holy Ghost always be near to help me, especially in trying times?

I felt myself becoming more and more distant from the gospel, so I turned away from the Church and the Lord, wanting to figure it out on my own. I wanted to know all of the answers to the questions that were building up inside me without the help of the gospel.

I had built a crumbling mindset in which I told myself I couldn't constantly rely on the Lord's help for seeking the answers I needed. So instead of asking the Lord my questions, I asked friends, parents, teachers, and anyone else I could think of. I had become eager to aspire and succeed, but when I attended church and Church activities, I felt like I was putting on a mask. Behind that mask was a struggling daughter of God being burned up by questions and by knowledge of what I thought was right and wrong.

I was lost. And I was having difficulty grasping the gospel. I felt

> *Divine nature. Eternal destiny. Daughter of God. Disciple of Jesus Christ. I didn't feel a connection with these words. I was able to say the words, but as they left my mouth, they were disconnected from my thoughts and seemed only part of a routine. I didn't know how to connect them* to *me.*

scared that I would completely lose my faith in what I had been taught. When I was questioning my own faith, I felt guilty since I had promised to always keep myself steady, learning Christ's words and teaching others along the way. How could I be an example to others when I wasn't even sure of the teachings of the gospel?

> *To be able to keep a steady and firm hand on the gospel, I started to surround myself with people who I knew believed in the Lord. . . . I asked questions I wanted the answers to and eventually began to find what I needed to hold onto my faith, increase my faith, and even apply it to my testimony.*

To be able to keep a steady and firm hand on the gospel, I started to surround myself with people who I knew believed in the Lord. When attending church, I partook in the lesson and shared with others my thoughts on the lesson for the week. I asked questions I wanted the answers to and eventually began to find what I needed to hold onto my faith, increase my faith, and even apply it to my testimony. Bit by bit, the false mindset I had built was slowly being brought down. I had glimpses of myself as a daughter of God. The words of the Young Women Theme began to have some meaning for me.

As my faith and understanding of how to live the gospel increased, so did my experiences that helped build my testimony. I was given the opportunity to serve in my ward Young Women on multiple occasions. As the president of my class, I planned weekly activities and attended meetings with other youth presidents of my ward with the bishop. There we would discuss upcoming activities and things we had learned through serving in our callings. I was able to strengthen the young women in my class and age group, as well as teach younger sisters about living and learning the gospel. These opportunities of responsibility have increased my testimony.

I was finally finding peace within myself, knowing the Lord had given me the opportunity to expand my faith in the gospel and nourish my testimony through ministering to others and helping them grow their own testimonies. However, even though I was growing and exercising my faith in the Lord, I was again surrounding myself with people who caused me to question my choice to live the gospel. As the president of my Young Women class, I felt tremendous guilt for wanting to know the answers to my never-ending sea of questions, many of which came from people around me. I felt wrong asking the Lord when I had already received so many answers. Why did I want to learn more? Why couldn't I be satisfied with the teachings I had consumed? I prayed to God daily and asked of Him to forgive my sins for pursuing more. In return, I was given forgiveness and clarity that I only wanted assurance of what I had been taught. The faults I had found within myself helped to increase my testimony and faith in the Lord, and I used them to approach Him. I was learning with all my heart to trust in the Lord and not lean upon my own understanding and to acknowledge Him in all my ways so that He would guide my path.[1]

> *I was finally finding peace within myself, knowing the Lord had given me the opportunity to expand my faith in the gospel and nourish my testimony through ministering to others and helping them grow their own testimonies.*

As I grew older and learned more of the word of God, my faith and testimony continued to enlarge. I completed my Personal Progress in the Young Women program. When I was given my certificate of completion, I felt the satisfaction of achievement. I felt more peace too. And it wasn't because of the certificate; it was the work I had done.

Later in the year, I participated in the yearly stake Young Women Camp. I asked myself if I really wanted to be there and be part of the

---

1. See Proverbs 3:5–6: "Trust in the Lord with all thine heart; and lean not unto thine own understanding. In all thy ways acknowledge Him, and he shall direct thy paths."

group, but I attended anyway. Attending that camp was one of the best experiences I've had in the Church. We participated in a variety of difficult tasks that tested our trust in the Lord and each other. Being surrounded by many young women who believed in living the gospel helped to increase my confidence, trust, and faith in the gospel and its teachings.

While at camp, we were challenged to make space for the Lord. We were asked: "What does it mean to make space for Him? What does it mean when we apply His teachings to our lives?" I learned that making space for Him means inviting the gospel and the Lord's teachings into our homes, families, and daily lives. It means I make time in the day to ponder on His teachings and on my faith. By learning to make space for Heavenly Father and Jesus Christ, I was learning to open up my heart, my soul, and my mind to the word of God. Making space for Him a little each day can make all the difference in the end! It did for me at camp, and it continues to do so now.

Making space for Him means inviting the gospel and the Lord's teachings into our homes, families, and daily lives. It means I make time in the day to ponder on His teachings and on my faith. By learning to make space for Heavenly Father and Jesus Christ, I was learning to open up my heart, my soul, and my mind to the word of God. Making space for Him a little each day can make all the difference in the end!

I bear testimony that the Lord and His gospel are how we successfully increase the Light of Christ in our lives and understand and apply the word of God. I believe that Christ is near, to strengthen us along the way, to grant forgiveness when we seek it, and to grant clarity when we are in the wrong. I strongly believe that the Holy Ghost was sent by the Lord to guide us on the path of discipleship. I believe that through living and learning the word of God, we are able to strengthen our testimonies, to increase our understanding of the teachings of Christ, to learn from and understand the scriptures, and to expand our faith in Christ.

It is a gift that God has bestowed on us to seek for repentance and to ask for forgiveness in this world where we have been given agency. I believe that Heavenly Father gave us the gift to make the decision to move forward in learning of Christ through personal revelation, and to use our testimonies to help and bless and sustain others in faith.

Entering the Young Women program helped me learn how to live the gospel and grow my faith and taught me that, while I learn and grow, I can still minister to others and thereby help the Lord while I am here on this earth. I have learned the importance of taking one step at a time. I tried to run too fast when I first entered Young Women, and I fumbled and stumbled. As I slowed down and built a foundation of faith in Christ under me, I felt on firmer ground. And I have learned that "living the gospel does not mean the storms of life will pass us by, but we will be better prepared to face them with serenity and peace."[2]

---

2. Joseph B. Wirthlin, "Finding a Safe Harbor," *Ensign*, May 2000.

HERITAGE AND LEGACY

J. TEKULVĒ JACKSON-VANN

J. Tekulvē Jackson-Vann is a native of Milledgeville, Georgia. He has a BS in marriage, family, and human development from Brigham Young University and an MS in marriage and family therapy from Valdosta State University. Tekulvē currently resides in Utah, is a father to four children, and is a doctoral student in the School of Medicine and Health Sciences at The George Washington University.

My journey to membership in The Church of Jesus Christ of Latter-day Saints began long before two missionaries ever knocked on my door. It began at birth. Being born with certain spiritual sensitivities, while my friends played video games and other typical childhood activities, I would sit in the house writing out sermons that I would then deliver to friends in my sister's playhouse, which I temporarily converted into a church. I would stand behind some piece of furniture dressed in the blue robe that I had been given for my kindergarten graduation and preach my written sermons. Early in life, I had earned the nickname "Reb" from family members. I had received the witness in my heart that God had called me to preach His gospel.

By the time I was nine, I had become aware that something was missing in our spiritual experiences as members of El Bethel Missionary Baptist Church. I commented to my mother that there was too much preaching and not enough teaching. I was not leaving Sunday services feeling like I had any new knowledge of God, His will for me, or my part in His plan. As a result, we stopped attending church, and I would give sermons to my family at home in the living room on Sunday mornings. After a while I had no new material to preach, and in my nine-year-old mind, my sermons were becoming repetitive. One evening in November of 1989, that would all change.

We gathered as we often did in my mother's room to chat before heading to bed. That night my mother asked us, "Have you ever wondered about where we came from, why we're here, and where we're going?" The subject matter piqued my interest, and we talked at length until we decided that the best option was to have a family prayer to find the answers.

The next day, two young White boys in white shirts and ties knocked on our door. This was uncommon in our neighborhood, but my sister and I had previously briefly talked to missionaries in the street one day while we were rehearsing our lines for a play. They had been a captive audience, so we had some level of respect for them. These two men introduced themselves as missionaries from The Church of Jesus Christ of Latter-day Saints. Then, as if he had known, one of them said, "We are in the area today sharing a message about where we came from, why we're here, and where we're going." I must have pulled him into the house with all of my strength! We spoke briefly with them, and they left a card for us to contact them if we wanted them to return.

After several days of debating in the family, my older brothers decided that they were not interested in hearing more. But I was sold, and my mother agreed to have them return if only to satisfy my curiosity. As they returned to teach, their message felt both new and exciting and familiar and comforting. With little resistance, my mother, sister, and I were baptized on Wednesday, January 30, 1990, in the Macon Georgia Stake Center as members of the Milledgeville Ward. Subsequently, I grew up attending that ward.

Early in life, I had earned the nickname "Reb" from family members. I had received the witness in my heart that God had called me to preach His gospel.

While my journey into the Church was easy, my path to staying has required a connection to heaven that I never knew I needed. In some way, I believe that a part of what makes the Church true is that I belong to it. In my mind, if Heavenly Father had so lovingly sent the gospel to me, He must really want me to have it.

I stay because my membership is a gift from Heavenly Father that I don't want to return or allow anyone to take from me. I stay because the gospel in its fullness offers me the greatest degree of hope that the suffering of this life has not been in vain and that my willingness to endure it well in this life will result in eternal blessings and joy in the life to come. I stay because I realize that I am the link between my ancestors who were denied the blessings of the gospel during their lifetimes and my descendants who will be born into the covenant and know that theirs is a spiritual birthright that none can deny them. I stay in hopes of being a part of the changes that must surely be coming in order for the Church to be a welcoming place for all.

> *I am the link between my ancestors who were denied the blessings of the gospel during their lifetimes and my descendants who will be born into the covenant and know that theirs is a spiritual birthright that none can deny them. I stay in hopes of being a part of the changes that must surely be coming in order for the Church to be a welcoming place for all.*

Staying has required me to be a pioneer in these latter days. I was blessed to be among the first Black Americans called to serve as an ordinance worker in the Payson Utah Temple. While serving there, I was able to be part of the change that allowed male workers to wear cultural hairstyles. I was blessed to serve as Young Men president of the Genesis Group for nearly seven years. I have also been blessed to spread the gospel as part of the Debra Bonner Unity Gospel Choir.

However, for every pioneering step, there have been moments that have challenged me to reach deeper into the roots of my testimony.

I've seen Cumorah's Hill. I've knelt in the Sacred Grove. I've walked the streets of Nauvoo. I've discovered the histories of ancestors who walked the trails from Nauvoo to the Salt Lake Valley. I've looked at my extended family history and seen the names of prophets, apostles, and pioneers and knew that I belonged. Yet my heart aches when I wonder if all of me belongs. Do I cling to my pioneer pedigree in order to legitimize my belonging? Would I feel as connected if all those names belonged to non–Latter-day Saint pioneers?

Most importantly of all, I stay because my patriarchal blessing tells me that mine is the responsibility of the tribe of Ephraim to prepare the earth for the Second Coming of Christ. He sought me out from the darkness of the world and put me on the path of gospel light. So I keep pressing forward, with faith in every footstep.

I KNOW THE WORK IS OF GOD

JOHN WESLEY HARMON JR.
1881–1940; baptized 1900

John Wesley Harmon (known as Wesley) was born in Warwick, Delaware, the oldest of four children born to John Wesley Harmon Sr. and Amelia Ann Street. Wesley graduated from James Logan School in Philadelphia in June 1900. On July 15, 1900, at the age of nineteen, Wesley was baptized into the Church. He owned and operated a flour mill in Sussex County, Delaware. On April 22, 1907, Wesley married Lillian Blanche Clark, daughter of William Russell Clark (Chief Wyniaco, head of the Nanticoke Tribe at the Indian River District in Sussex County) and Florence Drain. Wesley taught school in Delaware County, Pennsylvania. In 1914 he graduated with a bachelor of science degree from Delaware State College for Colored Students, now known as Delaware State University. He attended Howard University in Washington, DC, and during the 1917–18 school year, he received the ten-dollar prize in gold for the highest average over 85% in first-year Greek. He graduated in 1918. In the yearbook it is noted that he was "quiet, unassuming, and likable." Wesley owned a successful grocery store on Twelfth and S Streets in Washington, DC, which thrived for about twenty years, from approximately 1919 to 1939; it was one of the few Black American–owned businesses that survived past its first year.[1]

---

1. Justin Bray, "Harmon, John Wesley Jr. Biography," Century of Black Mormons, accessed September 4, 2021, https://exhibits.lib.utah.edu/s/century-of-black-mormons/page/harmon-john-wesley-jr#; Howard University Catalogue 1917–1918, Vol. XII No. 3, April 1918. Exhibit number five; "Native Americans of Delaware State," http://nativeamericansofdelawarestate.com/Mitsawokett%20Photos/HarmonSacajawea.htm; Harry B. Anderson "Meet Your Neighbor"; Washington Afro American, July 1, 1939; "If Walls Could Talk: The Coffee Bar—The Harmon Family Grocery Store (and full house)"; The Ghosts of DC, February 4, 2013, accessed September 4, 2021, https://ghostsofdc.org/2013/02/04/if-walls-could-talk-the-coffee-bar/.

I KNOW THE WORK IS OF GOD

I wish to add my testimony to those of the scattered Saints throughout the land. I was baptized July 15, 1900, since which time the blessing of the Lord has rested upon me in such a degree that I know the work is of God. Spread this fact to all the world: "Mormonism" is Truth![2]

---

2. Transcript is from *Liahona, The Elders' Journal* (June 20, 1908): 20. M205.5 L693 v. 5-42 1907–1945. Church History Library, The Church of Jesus Christ of Latter-day Saints; in the public domain.

TESTIMONY OF AN AGED ANCESTOR ON BEING BANNED FROM THE HOLY PRIESTHOOD

There is something sacred and divine in our **PAIN**,
I've thought since a lil boy,
'cause from it can come beauty, insight, wisdom, and creation.
I saw it with each child my Thressa birthed.
In her tears.
And in the couldn'ts placed on me.
In our pain is where we meet **JESUS**
in a segregated space that only such can enter.
In such a space I learned the Truth of who I am.
There in Mama's belly
I grew on greens n fried chicken n gravied rice.
'N **THE WORD OF GOD** which Mama also ate.
It became part of her. Part of me too.
I learned of God then.

You see . . .
I've known God since I was a teeny seed.
He was put into my bones when they were bein' formed.
His **TRUTH** runs through my veins with the blood my heart pumps.
So to tell me "less than" butts-against the Truth in me.
I reject it. I must.
For to accept it is not just accepting False
but **LYIN'** in The Light of God that gives me Life.
That gives me Sight.
That is in my every Breath.
Less than is *ME*, you say?
No, sir!
I am God's own.
God never made **ANYTHING** that was less than glorious or divine.
Divine is what I am, you see,
'cause I am God's **OWN**.

—*Alice Faulkner Burch*

THE BICYCLE TRIP

RANDY CUTLIFF AND DENISE SILVA

Randy Cutliff is married and resides in Utah. He volunteers in the local community and has had many callings, including executive secretary and third counselor of the Genesis Group, ward mission leader, ward membership clerk, elders quorum counselor, elders quorum president, ward clerk, Sunday School counselor, and currently, Sunday School teacher.

Denise Silva lives in Minnesota with her husband and children and works in human resources, equity, and inclusion. Her callings have included full-time missionary in the Spain Malaga Mission, Sunday School teacher, and Relief Society teacher. She has also served in ward and stake Relief Society presidencies. She enjoys being on the board of directors for nonprofit organizations.

RANDY'S START

I am disheartened when I hear of traumatizing events that cause Black people to feel uncomfortable while living an earthly life. This feeling is what led me to seek comfort by embracing the Lord's Church. My children and I were baptized on February 11, 1995, in Michigan.

My complete conversion, however, materialized several months following my family's baptism, while I was traveling with my sixteen-year-old daughter Denise in Tarragona, Spain. During this trip, Denise received inspiration that she should read the entirety of 3 Nephi of the Book of Mormon. After two weeks in Spain, she decided to rent a bicycle and go on a sightseeing trip. Denise told me about the parallels between her sightseeing trip and Heavenly Father's plan for all of us. Her story changed my life forever.

DENISE'S BICYCLE TRIP

My earthly father provided me with everything I needed to take a bicycle ride in a foreign country and safely return back to the hotel. The night before, I used a map to plan the trip and highlighted the route, which included a rest stop at a glorious park at the end of the long journey. My father gave me money and encouraged me to buy whatever I needed to have a safe and enjoyable trip.

In comparison, Heavenly Father has given us everything we need to make our earthly journey and safely return home. At the end of our journey, we will have the opportunity to rest with Him in His kingdom. The plan of salvation shows us the path we can follow to return to live with Him.

As I was renting the bicycle, I was asked if I also wanted a helmet and elbow and knee pads. I decided to save the money my earthly father had given me, so I declined getting the personal-protection equipment. Since I knew how to ride a bicycle, I didn't think I needed it.

We do the same thing with the time our Heavenly Father provides us. It is natural for us to say that we don't have the time to read the scriptures, pray, watch general conference, or go to church or the temple, even though we know these things will bring us the protection we need for our journey on earth.

Heavenly Father has given us everything we need to make our earthly journey and safely return home.

On my bicycle journey, I passed many forks in the road, but I wasn't tempted to go down any of those paths. I was determined to stay on the path I had outlined. In life some things don't tempt us as much as others. Those temptations are easy for us to avoid.

After a while, I came to a fork in the road that was particularly inviting. I stopped to look at the map. The map indicated I should take the path on the left, but the path on the right looked like it would provide more sights to see. Since I figured it would be impossible for me to get lost in such a small city, I ventured down the path on the right and quickly found that it truly was a beautiful route to take. The scenery looked like a picture postcard with farmland and rolling hills.

On our earthly journey, we often make decisions to take a route that is off the chosen path. Why? Because it seems the detour will be a pleasant journey where we can partake of scenery and items that will be pleasing to our eyes and body.

I began riding fast, up and down the rolling hills, twisting and turning around curving paths. It was so much fun! Then I began to realize that I had traveled too far off my plotted path. I could no longer see the main road. I had taken so many twists and turns that I couldn't remember the way back. There were no homes in sight and there was no one on the road. I realized I hadn't seen a house or other people in a long time. I panicked and turned my bike around.

In fear, I pedaled as fast I could to try to find my way back home. At top speed, I came around a corner that immediately led to a sharp downhill slope and a large rock in the middle of my path that I couldn't avoid at the speed I was traveling. I hit the rock and flipped over the bicycle. I am sure that I blacked out for a second, after which I became aware of my surroundings. I noticed that the bicycle's frame was bent, my shorts were torn and dirty, blood was oozing out of my knees, my bare elbows were dirty and scratched, and blood was running down one of my elbows. I was scared and confused because I knew that it would not be easy for me to get back to the hotel and I could not imagine returning in my current condition. I was so sad that I began to cry.

The adversary puts obstacles along our earthly routes because he wants us to get hurt and continue making decisions that are contrary to Heavenly Father's plan. Satan wants us to make decisions that lead us off the strait and narrow path, and then he wants us to continue making poor decisions, hoping we will become insensitive to the newly created misery. Even though we sometimes step off the path that was planned by Heavenly Father, His love for us is unchanging. Heavenly Father is always listening for our sincere prayers so that He can provide inspiration and guidance to help us return to the path.

I then remembered a Young Women lesson about the power of prayer. I prayed to Heavenly Father for help and inspiration. As I finished the prayer, I heard the sound of an approaching motorcycle.

Through scripture, Heavenly Father makes the repeated promise, "Ask, and it shall be given unto you; seek, and ye shall find; knock, and it shall be opened unto you. For every one that asketh, receiveth; and he that seeketh, findeth; and to him that knocketh, it shall be opened" (3 Nephi 14:7–8).

I looked up and saw a policeman on the motorcycle. He was different than any policemen I had ever seen. His motorcycle was black and shiny. I could not see his face because the visor on his helmet was very dark. He stopped next to me, turned off the motor, and raised the visor. He said, "I saw what happened. Can I help you?"

Heavenly Father does not abandon us when we make poor decisions. He looks for our humility and repentance. All we need to do is sincerely ask for His comfort and help. He will send the Holy Spirit, a comforter to guide us back onto the path.

> *Even though we sometimes step off the path that was planned by Heavenly Father, His love for us is unchanging. Heavenly Father is always listening for our sincere prayers so that He can provide inspiration and guidance to help us return to the path.*

I looked at the policeman. I doubted that he could carry me on his motorcycle with a bent bicycle. In a soft voice, I answered, "No."

The policeman asked again, "Are you sure that I cannot help you?"

I responded, "Yes, I am sure."

He said, "Okay," then pulled down his visor, started his motorcycle, and drove down one of the many alleys.

My head immediately dropped, and I thought it was very foolish of me not to let him help. Then I had another thought: the policeman seems like he knows where he is going, so maybe I should follow him. I followed where the policeman went. I walked less than a quarter of a mile, and to my surprise I came to the street where my hotel was located.

The Holy Spirit is Heavenly Father's guiding light for us to follow on our way back to the chosen path. He will always show us how to return to Heavenly Father's plan and helps us, regardless of how far off the path we have strayed. The help of the Holy Spirit can appear in many forms, and to me it was a policeman on a shiny motorcycle. I was able to find the route back to the hotel by following the path that he had taken.

I started walking to the hotel and I began to notice people who were walking toward me. Before they reached me, they would cross over the street and walk on the other side. I then noticed that they would return to the side of the street that I was on after they had passed by me. I thought that this was very wise of them because there I was: a Black girl on a street in Tarragona with torn clothes, covered in dirt and blood and walking with a bent bicycle frame. I began to feel lonely and sad.

As we take steps to return to Heavenly Father's path, people may notice that we are unclean and will avoid us. This can distract and deter us from returning to the strait and narrow path. But our main objective and focus must be to continue forward.

Then two little girls, who were around the ages of four and six, approached me with their mother. They walked right up to me and said, "Hola!"

I ignored them, and once again they said, "Hola, señorita!"

I finally smiled at them and replied, "Hola!"

They returned my smile and then skipped to their mother to continue their journey.

Heavenly Father has also provided us with saints. These saints will help cheer us up and encourage us to stay on the route that leads us back to the strait and narrow path, where we can once again become clean and return home to be with our Heavenly Father.

RANDY'S COMPLETE CONVERSION

Denise was edified by the Holy Spirit to the extent that I too was touched by the Holy Spirit and became energized by the Lord and inspired by His eternal and unchangeable gospel. My comprehension of the true Church became self-evident a few years later when Denise opened her missionary calling letter and found that the Lord had called her to serve in Spain, the place from whence His everlasting seed of knowledge had been planted and fertilized.

> *The Holy Spirit is Heavenly Father's guiding light for us to follow on our way back to the chosen path. He will always show us how to return to Heavenly Father's plan and helps us, regardless of how far off the path we have strayed.*

THE GOSPEL IS HERE ON EARTH

FRANCES ANN STEWART HOOD
1832–1910

Frances Ann Stewart Hood was born in Greenfield, Ohio, and was the eighth of ten children born to Richard Stewart and Barbara Creacy Stewart. She is descended from members of the Sapponi and Pamunkey Tribes of Virginia and from the formerly enslaved Africans who were welcomed into those tribes. She married Josiah Hood on October 11, 1860, in Cass County, Michigan. They had six children, plus three from Josiah's previous marriage. Frances raised nine children total. Frances was converted to the gospel when her son George Little Berry Hood shared with her a remarkable dream he had. At the age of sixty-eight, Frances was baptized in the Christiana Creek in Cass County with her son and his wife. She was a member of the Church branch in South Bend, Indiana, when she passed.[1]

I[2] was baptized August 25, 1901 . . . and I know that a man must be called as was Aaron to preach the gospel, and that apostles and prophets must remain in the Church until we all come to the unity of the faith. John the Revelator saw an angel earthward bound bearing the gospel, which I believe is here on the earth.[3]

---

1. Ardis E. Parshall, "Hood, Frances Ann Stewart," Century of Black Mormons, University of Utah, accessed July 16, 2021, https://exhibits.lib.utah.edu/s/century-of-black-mormons/page/hood-frances-ann-stewart.
2. Excerpt from *Liahona, the Elders' Journal* 6 (August 8, 1908): 191, Church History Library, The Church of Jesus Christ of Latter-day Saints. Public domain.
3. See Revelation 14:6–7: "And I saw another angel fly in the midst of heaven, having the everlasting gospel to preach unto them that dwell on the earth, and to every nation, and kindred, and tongue, and people, Saying with a loud voice, Fear God, and give glory to him; for the hour of his judgment is come: and worship him that made heaven, and earth, and the sea, and the fountains of waters."

I FOUND A BROTHER

EARL JOSEPH HUNTER JR.

Earl Joseph Hunter Jr. is seventy-six years old and has been a member of the Church for forty-two years. A farm boy, he grew up with a strong Christian family background. Earl has served the United States as a soldier in the Vietnam War and has served many years in the educational system as a school board member. He currently resides in Richmond, Virginia.

My life circumstances have exposed me to a number of diverse cultures and religions. Knowing the fullness of the gospel, I have felt that there was more teaching and living that each of us should be responsible for, and it has been like a new birth to me.

My journey within The Church of Jesus Christ of Latter-day Saints started during the summer of 1972. One day I was traveling with my brother-in-law, his brother-in-law, and our wives to Northern Virginia/Maryland to attend a musical concert. We crested the top of a hill on Interstate I-495 going west, and this big building with a majestic, large, gold statue appeared in the middle of the highway. I asked my brother-in-law, "What is that?" The only answer he gave was, "It belongs to a church, but I don't know more about it." From that day forward, each time I visited Maryland and returned home, I took the same route so I could take in that view.

I met with my three friends and business partners regularly each Tuesday evening, until one evening our leader missed our meeting. My friend Stuart Scott and I eventually found out he was meeting with missionaries from The Church of Jesus Christ of Latter-day Saints.

Sometime later he asked us to attend his baptism. We wondered if he was trying to get us to also join his new church, but we attended anyway. Approximately a year later, in 1980, I was asked if missionaries could come visit with my family.

I grew up with very strong historical family ties, roots, and a foundation in the Baptist faith. I had gone to church every Sunday for as long as I could remember, and my family and I typically attended all services and meetings outside of Sundays, including special events and celebrations within my church and other Baptist churches in the community. My grandparents were strong participants in the church. Grandfather Deacon Lucian O. Hunter was the first person to purchase a bus so countless youth in Hanover, Virginia, could attend the local training center during the 1930s. My father, Earl Joseph Hunter Sr., was the superintendent of Sunday school for more than fifteen years, a deacon, and the church treasurer, among other positions to support the church. My mother Pearl V. Hunter was the oldest deaconess, sang in the choir, and served in many other ministries as well.

Following in the footsteps of such great examples instilled a life of service in me. With solid ties to church, family, and a church family to support me, I regularly attended Sunday school, ushered, sang in the choir, became a trustee, and served to support the school system. Yet even with my strong connection to the Baptist church, I accepted the request for a visitation from the missionaries. After their first visit, they continued to visit me and my family in our home weekly.

During our weekly discussions, the two sister missionaries opened the door to a greater understanding of what I had previously envisioned about the Lord Jesus Christ. They helped me become much more aware of my obligation for the gift of the sacrifice of Jesus and His restored gospel. Before this, I had only thoughts that I had embraced and held within my heart, but being a husband and father, I acutely knew that I needed to be an example to and for my family. Getting away from my military style of living and being taught the fullness of the gospel could not have come at a better time.

In 1980, after approximately four months of reading, praying, learning, and pondering, I could not deny what I had learned and felt in my heart and spirit. After a few lessons the missionaries asked me to give up smoking, and I did so with conviction and no difficulty. My wife was also on board, and my two older children were progressing within their studies of the gospel. We attended church services and found them to be tranquil and comforting. Truly, we were not accustomed to three different hour-long sessions, but the actual number of hours spent at church were approximately the same amount of time we had spent attending the Baptist church. Being one of few African Americans was customary anywhere I went. It was something I faced daily as a US Army officer as well as a helicopter pilot. My commissioned rank of captain and earned assignments meant that, during my entire military life, I was always in an environment where I was one of the only African Americans. That's why not seeing other African Americans in the Church didn't upset me or turn me away.

> *The two sister missionaries opened the door to a greater understanding of what I had previously envisioned about the Lord Jesus Christ. They helped me become much more aware of my obligation for the gift of the sacrifice of Jesus and His restored gospel.*

My youngest son had just been born when our missionaries, Sister Sandra Graham and her companion, presented us with the challenge to be baptized. In December 1980 my wife and I became confirmed members of the Richmond Ward, and I was immediately ordained to the Aaronic Priesthood. I invited my friend Stuart to attend my baptism as well as church services. He soon accepted and began visiting with the missionaries in his home.

The next year—1981—was an even bigger year in my life. I baptized my daughter in January, and then I baptized my good friend

Stuart. I was also ordained an elder. Later that year my family and I drove to the Washington D.C. Temple, located about one hundred miles from our home, to be sealed. The youngest children vomited all morning because of nerves, but by the time they were brought into the sealing room they were feeling well and were happy. I finally entered the beautiful building I had admired years ago, and we became an eternal family. Though my understanding of the Book of Mormon was small at that time, I firmly believed in Joseph Smith's First Vision. Learning all about the priesthood and its responsibilities was a lot of effort, but I looked forward to it. I worked very hard to get my temple recommend and to get my family sealed that first year.

I finally entered the beautiful building I had admired years ago, and we became an eternal family.

I have remained very thankful for the sister missionaries who taught me and the number of families who took us under their wings, providing counsel, nurture, and guidance. Jim and Pat Huber became our first "Grateful Family," inviting my family to their home for a cookout and pool party, their daughter becoming the babysitter and swim instructor for our two younger sons. Our home teacher became and has remained a great friend, and Stuart has remained my spiritual brother all these years. I have also remained great friends with the families I have ministered to along my journey. These connections bless and enrich my life.

My first Church calling required that I get to sacrament meeting thirty minutes before services began. I was given the charge of plugging in the microphone and making sure it properly functioned at the sacrament table. This was a simple and easy calling but an essential one that made sacrament meeting easier for the bishopric. Since then, I have held multiple positions within the Sunday School and elders quorum. I was also assigned as the executive secretary for a number of years. At our new Mechanicsville Ward building, I also enjoyed working on projects such as painting, staining interior wood, and helping install the underground irrigation system. My family and I have been blessed to engage in many community outreach opportunities over the years. In my early years as a member, I also participated on our ward softball team, the only Latter-day Saint team in the community. Playing teams from other churches helped in building good relationships between the different churches.

I have been blessed to attend a number of Church functions where I was able to shake hands with a number of the General Authorities of the Church. For instance, in 1985 my sons were in the Boy Scouts of America, and we attended the Boy Scouts Jamboree at Fort A.P. Hill, Virginia, where President Ezra Taft Benson, a member of the Quorum of the Twelve Apostles at the time, was the speaker. More recently, in 2019, Elder Gary E. Stevenson of the Quorum of the Twelve Apostles was the keynote speaker at a large NAACP function in Washington, DC, where I was able to shake hands with him. He asked of me, "How long have you been a member?" I replied, "Thirty-nine years." He then hugged me and rubbed cheeks with me.

I am seventy-six years old now. For the past four years I have attended the Legacy of LDS Black Pioneers conference

> *Being obedient to all the commitments I have made to my Heavenly Father is very important to me. Prayerfully, I strive to maintain and improve each day of my mortality. I thank Heavenly Father for sending His Son to pay my debts of sin. As I do my best, I pray that I will always be worthy to carry a temple recommend.*

at the Washington, DC, Visitors' Center. There I met with the most prominent African American brothers of the Church. Being able to hear speakers from other states and from Church headquarters, to learn about the African American history within the Church, and to connect with other African American members have enlarged my soul and increased my understanding and enlightenment. All these experiences have buoyed me up, contributing to my feeling that I belong and to my enjoyment in my life.

Being obedient to all the commitments I have made to my Heavenly Father is very important to me. Prayerfully, I strive to maintain and improve each day of my mortality. I thank Heavenly Father for sending His Son to pay my debts of sin. As I do my best, I pray that I will always be worthy to carry a temple recommend. I have mostly enjoyed my journey and most of what I have learned from it. My spiritual brother Stuart has remained my brother all these years.

POURED FROM THE HAND OF GOD

RANDALL SILAS

Randall Silas was born August 1965 to William and Margie Silas. He grew up in Hattiesburg, Mississippi, where he met and married his high school sweetheart, Betty. Joining the Church in December 1992, they have been members for thirty years. Randall works as a radiologic technologist, and he and Betty have five children and eleven grandchildren and still reside in Hattiesburg.

While serving as the first African American bishop in the Hattiesburg Mississippi Stake, I experienced and witnessed several miracles. I share two miracles that I personally experienced with you now.

MIRACLE #1

Two years before being called as bishop, I had an impression that the Lord wanted me to become a bishop. I had served Him in several callings over the years, including in three different bishoprics. Those callings had prepared me; however, being bishop would be different. I was called to lead and set a good example for all within the ward boundaries inside and outside the Church.

Prior to receiving this impression, I had decided to go back to school full time so I could make a career change, since I was then only working part time. By the time the call came, I was working two jobs in my new career field and preparing to financially assist two of my children to fulfill their desire of becoming full-time missionaries. Although they had both worked to put away some money to cover the cost of a mission, it wasn't nearly enough.

Within two months of my call as bishop, they were on a plane together heading to the MTC in Provo, Utah. Shortly after that I took on a third job to assist covering their mission cost. Although one of my nonmember family members committed to donate monthly to the missions, and other family and fellow Church members gave when they could, the total amount still fell short of what was needed. Unknowingly to me, one of my counselors in the bishopric reached out to his parents, who lived in another state and who reached out to their ward members to assist my children. Within a few weeks, money to cover the cost of my children's missions was received. It was an enormous blessing and miracle that would bless me and my children. Not only did this blessing lighten my load financially, but it allowed me more time to fully lead and give more time as bishop, thereby blessing the ward I was serving. Within a month of receiving this miracle, I was able to say goodbye to my coworkers at my third job.

> *I'm grateful that Heavenly Father answered the prayers of a bishop and a man who believed. In His acknowledgment of us and our needs, God had reached out His hand and poured forth miracles upon us.*

MIRACLE #2

During a ward council meeting, it was determined that the roof of one Church member's home was in dire need of repair. Plans were made for evaluations to be done; to look into the resources of the ward member, their family, and our community; and to check the cost of materials. Once the plans had been completed, the ward council scheduled the project to take place over a two-day period. The old, damaged roof would be removed on a Friday afternoon and evening, and then repair work and laying down the new roof would take place the next day.

At the conclusion of Friday night, all the workers had given much.

The Holy Spirit led me to thank each person there for what we had been able to accomplish and to gather everyone together in a word of prayer. I felt the Holy Spirit giving me the words to pray; other than asking Heavenly Father to protect the home, I don't remember much of what I said. After getting home and cleaning up, I sat down to watch the news. The forecast was for rain throughout the night in our area. I looked at my wife and said, "Looks like I'm going to have to go get some tarps and go back to the house we're repairing." Right after I said that, I heard God's voice say to me, "Where is your faith, Bishop? Didn't you just ask me to protect that house?" With that, I chose not to go to the store to buy tarps.

After saying my personal prayer for the night, I went to bed. The next morning I noticed that rain had fallen at my house. Saying to myself, "It's too late now. It is what it is," I went to the home we were repairing. Upon arrival, there was no sign of rain at all. Neither the house nor any of the supplies nor any of the ground around were wet. As others arrived, they too noticed that nothing was wet, even though they had all had rain at their homes. The house didn't get any of the forecasted rain until after the last shingle was laid that afternoon.

God had heard the prayers I had offered to Him. He had sent people to help me do what I couldn't do alone in paying for my children to serve Him away from home. As further testimony of His mercy and kindness, He placed His Holy Spirit upon me to guide me in what to say to bless a family's home with protection. I'm grateful that Heavenly Father answered the prayers of a bishop and a man who believed. In His acknowledgment of us and our needs, God had reached out His hand and poured forth miracles upon us.

"Jesus is the Christ, the Eternal God; And that he manifesteth himself unto all those who believe in him, by the power of the Holy Ghost; yea, unto every nation, kindred, tongue, and people, working mighty miracles, signs, and wonders, among the children of men according to their faith" (2 Nephi 26:12–13).

I **KNOW** THE VOICE
OF MY JESUS

Editor's Note: This is not an actual interview. This creative narrative represents interviews with formerly enslaved persons. Seymon Robinson is not one of them. None of the interviews in the collection held at the Library of Congress mention either baptism or membership in The Church of Jesus Christ of Latter-day Saints. The interviewer, Helen Bowen, is a fictional character created by the poet. The term "Mormon Church" is used in the historical context of the time represented.

Private efforts to preserve the life histories of formerly enslaved persons accounted for a small portion of the narratives collected during the late 1920s and 1930s. The "Born in Slavery: Slave Narratives from the Federal Writers' Project, 1936–1938" is an actual project formally dispatched on April 1, 1937; South Carolina is one of the states included in the project. Although several formerly enslaved individuals and families remained in Utah (the headquarters of the Church), there are no narratives from the state of Utah. There were Black American interviewers assigned to the narratives project.

Interview: Time Stamp 45:10:00
Tape 2.

Helen Bowen, interviewer:
We're almost done, Mr. Seymon. This is Helen Bowen interviewing Mr. Seymon (Say-moan) Robinson in Beaufort, South Carolina, part of the Gullah Geechee People. He was born enslaved about 1828. He is 109 years old. Tape 1 covers his memories of his parents, his master,

and his life enslaved. Tape 2 covers him as a member of the Mormon Church. He was baptized into the Mormon Church in 1887. Today's date is 28 July 1937. This is tape 2 of 2.

I don't want this to be hard for you. I heard there was an incident where you were nearly killed. Because you're Black.

(long pause)

Seymon Robinson:
Yes'm.
Right afta ou baptism. Monf.
Wenta chuch Sunday n come home.
We was fixin ou meal n heah a noise.
She said dohn go out. I went out. I saw em.
Fi in dey hands.
Fixin ta buhn ou house down.
Tol me I dont have no Pries'hood.
But I have me faif in Jesus. She have stronga faif den me.
We prayed us a blessin ova ou house. Prayed it strong.
Da day dey come wid fi ta buhn it down.
Looky now. Dis house still heh. Yes yes!
Dey put fi n wont buhn. Dey try again. wont buhn.
Yes yes! Praise Jesus!
Erry time they put tha fi it wont buhn. Erry time.
Well, they got tied n lef. Yelled wuhds at us.
Dey wuhds drop dere on tha ground n washed away in da rain.
Dey neh come back.

Helen Bowen:
Some said there was an angel standing there blowing out the fire each time they touched it to your house.

People at church treated you differently. Was it because of how you speak too?

Seymon Robinson:

Mmm hmm.

My peopas aint stupid.

Dis'**ou** Geechee.

Dis'**ou** Ancestas.

Dis'how **we** talk.

My Ancestas jus as impotan as yone.

    (silence)

Was hahd.

I say **dat**.

Widout my faif in Jesus . . . widout Jesus
I couldna made it 'long.

But . . . ya know

(pause)

aint posta be easy.

Dat what Jesus said in showin us.

Helen Bowen:

What was the hardest part for you being a member?

Seymon Robinson:

Knowin from Jesus who I is,
wheh I stand wid him,
walkin wid him **erry** day,
but bein told by leadas n uddas
dat I aint bahely human.
Times I neah believe 'em!

(laugh)

I KNOW THE VOICE OF MY JESUS

Helen Bowen:
But you kept going anyway. You stayed a member anyway. Always did your assignment.

You're still active in the church today?

Seymon Robinson:
Sho did!
Yes, ma'am, still doin.

Helen Bowen:
How has your faith kept you going?

Seymon Robinson:
Ya know, da voice of Jesus . . .
Was **louda** erry day.
One day . . .
I sho it was my last . . .
Sho Da Good Lord was callin me Home.
Dis heh one man . . .

(pause)

dat how I's gon say who n all.
Well dis one man he was callin me names and sayin his say right in my **face**!
Tellin me I's stupid. Aint got no brain. Cant thank or put two togetta.
Bohn to be a slave. We always be slaves. We fought gainst Jesus in Hea'em.
And you know I heah the voice of Jesus **louda** den his in my ears. Jesus right dere truf tellin.

Helen Bowen:
Thank you for talking about your life as a member of the Mormon

Church.
I forgot to ask: how old were you when you were baptized?

Seymon Robinson:
Ya know . . .
it was like havin
God hisself in one ear
n Old Scratch in da udda.

Helen Bowen:
When that man said those things to you?

Seymon Robinson:
Mmm hmm. Mmm hmm.

(silence)

Two Angels peopa say we walk wid.
Good Angel on da right sholda.
Devil Angel on da left sholda.
But I **know** the voice of my Jesus.

(silence)

Helen Bowen:
How old were you when you were baptized?

Seymon Robinson:
Fiffty nine. Hunded nine now.
Mmm hmm!
Like Samuel when Da Lord kept a'callin him
and Eli had ta **tell** him who dat was.

(laugh)

Dat was me.
Had ta learn.

I KNOW THE VOICE OF MY JESUS

Had ta **learn to reka'nize** the voices.
Not erry voice dat speak ta us is from Jesus ya know.

Helen Bowen:
I know. I've learned that too.
What **one thing** would you say to young people today?

Seymon Robinson:
Dat der!
Not erry voice dat speak to ya is from Jesus . . .
or **knows** Jesus.
Learn who voice the voice is.

—*Alice Faulkner Burch*

TUNING MY HEART TO MY ANCESTORS

KINNITH E. HOLLOWAY

Kinnith Holloway grew up in Moss Point, Mississippi. He is married to Debbie Carswell and works as a tax accountant. Debbie and Kinnith converted to the Church in 2001 while living in Natchez, Mississippi. They are currently members of the Pleasant Grove Utah West Stake, where Kinnith serves as bishop.

I am Kinnith Holloway. I am the ninth of the nine children born of Webster and Anna Holloway. I never knew John and Mary Bell Holloway, my paternal grandparents. My father Webster died in January 2000. My mother Anna died in March 2000. They had been married for sixty-four years. They died less than thirty days apart, and their deaths were devastating for me. I was not a religious person but knew my parents had a strong belief in God, the Heavenly Father, and Jesus Christ. Although I was a student of religion, I wasn't a member of a particular church and held no belief in any religion.

One day two missionaries showed up at my home to share some information about Jesus Christ. I listened to them but had absolutely no interest in what they were sharing. They caught my attention when they told me that Joseph Smith saw God and Jesus Christ and that vision led to the Restoration of the gospel. I had always felt that if Jesus Christ did exist, He would have to restore His gospel because the concept of denominationalism had fragmented the gospel and its teachings, spreading them like shards upon the earth to the point that a restoration was required.

The Prophet Joseph mentioned that the messenger Moroni was sent from the presence of God to him (Joseph Smith—History 1:33), and the messenger taught him many things over the space of a time. Moroni quoted the scripture from Malachi 4:5–6, but with a difference. He said: "And again, he quoted the fifth verse thus: *Behold, I will reveal* unto you the Priesthood, by the hand of Elijah the prophet, before the coming of the great and dreadful day of the Lord. He also quoted the next verse differently: And he shall plant in the hearts of the children the promises made to the fathers, and the hearts of the children shall turn to their fathers. If it were not so, the whole earth would be utterly wasted at his coming" (Joseph Smith—History 1:38–39; emphasis added).

Later in an epistle to the Church, the Prophet Joseph explained that "it is sufficient to know, in this case, that the earth will be smitten with a curse unless there is a *welding link* of some kind or other between the fathers and the children" (Doctrine and Covenants 128:18; emphasis added).

Through the restored gospel, we now know that this is the genealogy work we have been asked to do. Because of this work, our ancestors are able to receive the saving and exalting ordinances. This is all related to the spirit of Elijah, which has been poured upon the earth. Prior to the Restoration of the gospel of Jesus Christ through the Prophet Joseph Smith, almost no one did genealogy work. Today almost everyone does genealogy work in some manner, even if they don't know why. All people are God's children, and upon all people is poured the spirit of Elijah. Our hearts have been tuned to our ancestors. Our ancestors' hearts

> *I had always felt that if Jesus Christ did exist, He would have to restore His gospel because the concept of denominationalism had fragmented the gospel and its teachings, spreading them like shards upon the earth to the point that a restoration was required.*

have been tuned to us to help us find them that we can be linked and welded together. Our ancestors want this as much as we do.

In 2000, the Holy Ghost whispered to me that I had been presented the restored gospel. On January 28, 2001, I accepted it into my life by baptism. Soon after, the spirit of Elijah came upon me, and my heart was tuned to my ancestors. Together my ancestors and I have sought out my lineage, me working on this side while they work on the other side of the veil.

I knew my father and mother, Webster and Anna. My father knew his parents, John and Mary Bell, and left their information for me. No one here knew my grandfather's father, Alex Holloway. I wasn't able to locate him until the day I was standing on the 155 acres that my Grandfather John had been given. That day I felt a prompting from the Holy Ghost to trace how this land came to him. I searched in the Jefferson Davis County Office in Mississippi but didn't find any records of the land ownership. It seemed a dead end until a woman at the county office told me that Jefferson Davis County didn't exist until 1909, and recommended I check Covington County. There in the Covington County land office I found the record! The land deed was in my hand! My grandfather John had received land from his father, my great-grandfather Alex Holloway. Great-grandfather Alex homesteaded the land according to the paper signed by US President James Garfield. That piece of paper was the missing clue I needed. With it I was able to learn of my ancestors and link myself to them.

I am Kinnith Holloway.

I am the son of Webster Holloway.

> *All people are God's children, and upon all people is poured the spirit of Elijah. Our hearts have been tuned to our ancestors. Our ancestors' hearts have been tuned to us to help us find them that we can be linked and welded together. Our ancestors want this as much as we do.*

I am the grandson of John Holloway.

I am the great-grandson of Alex Holloway, who was born enslaved to fifteen-year-old Silvia, who had been enslaved and raped by a White man.

I am the great-great-grandson of that same Silvia who was born enslaved in 1820 at the Fisher Plantation in North Carolina and who was sold to the Holloway Plantation in Tennessee. It was she who took the surname of Holloway for herself and her son Alex when they moved to Mississippi after being freed.

In 2000, I heard the message of the restored gospel from two sister missionaries. They taught me how to identify the Holy Ghost. From the Holy Ghost I have received the truth that I now hold in my life. The Holy Ghost bore witness to me that the gospel I was hearing from the missionaries was the true restored gospel of Jesus Christ. The Holy Ghost witnessed unto me that the Bible is true. The Holy Ghost witnessed unto me that the Book of Mormon is true. The Holy Ghost witnessed unto me that Joseph Smith Jr. was a prophet of God. The Holy Ghost witnessed unto me that I am one of the sons of God, the Heavenly Father, and one of the brothers of Jesus Christ.

ACKNOWLEDGMENTS

We are grateful to have this opportunity to contribute to this book with our stories and testimonies in our own voice. As the expressions of faith and hope of those Black American members of The Church of Jesus Christ of Latter-day Saints who went before us inspired those of us of this generation, may our expressions of faith and hope as Black American members of this generation inspire those in the next generation until we all come to sit down together in a unity of the Faith, filled with Love born of Hope for one another.

We thank the Daughters of Utah Pioneers for material and support cheerfully given; with special acknowledgments to Ellen Jepson, President; Constance Huntsman, Historian; and Pam Carson, Librarian. Thanks to all the contributing historians of the Century of Black Mormons database (housed by the University of Utah) for their research that made the research for this book easier by having so much Black American history contained in one location. Special thanks to historical researcher extraordinaire Ardis E. Parshall, whose gift of research brought into the light the words of Ms. Marie, and without whose gift we would not have them to read today.

We express gratitude to Laurel Christensen Day and Celia Barnes for their patience, kindness, support, and encouragement. This book wouldn't exist without them and their determination to change the tide of what has been to usher in a new day.

With love we thank our families and friends whose cheering and support saw us through the writing, editing, rewriting, and several re-edits to arrive at this final version.

The Jubilee Singers, 1873; in the public domain.

FURTHER READING

"Black History Timeline." Blacklatterdaysaints.org. Accessed April 18, 2022. http://www.blacklatterdaysaints.org/history.

This timeline produced by the Church presents a side-by-side historic overview of Black Americans in the United States generally and of Black Americans in the Church specifically.

Bonner, Chantel, and Mauli Junior Bonner. *A Child of God*. Salt Lake City: Deseret Book, 2021.

A children's book by husband and wife Mauli and Chantel Bonner, who share the importance of representation in Church books and artwork for Black American children.

Embry, Jessie L. *Black Saints in a White Church: Contemporary African American Mormons*. Salt Lake City: Signature Books, 1994.

This book provides a history of Blacks in the Church, drawing on a large number of oral histories that were part of "BYU's LDS African American Oral History Project," conducted by Alan Cherry, with Black American members across the United States from 1985 to the early 1990s.

Gray, Darius Aidan, and Margaret Blair Young. Standing on the Promises. Provo, Utah: Zarahemla Books, 2013.

This three-book series includes *Book 1: One More River to Cross*; *Book 2: Bound for Canaan*; and *Book 3: The Last Mile of the Way*. This trilogy provides an excellent historical overview of Black Americans in the Church.

"Race and the Priesthood." Gospel Topics Essays, The Church of Jesus Christ of Latter-day Saints. https://www.churchof

jesuschrist.org/study/manual/gospel-topics-essays/race-and-the-priesthood?lang=eng.

This essay reflects the Church's formal stance on the priesthood and temple restrictions and states that none of the theories advanced by many Church leaders and members to explain the restrictions are "accepted today as the official doctrine of the Church."

Reeve, W. Paul. *Religion of a Different Color: Race and the Mormon Struggle.* Oxford University Press, 2016.

This is an excellent book comprising historical research on the priesthood restriction, on early Black American men who held the priesthood, and on the points that led to the rescinding of the Church policy that lasted 126 years.

Vranes, Zandra, and Tamu Smith. *Can I Get an Amen? Celebrating the Lord in Everyday Life.* Salt Lake City: Deseret Book, 2019.

Zandra and Tamu are also known as the "Sistas in Zion." Their first book together reveals Black American culture as they share personal stories of walking the gospel path.

SOURCES AND CREDITS

Epigraph, p. 9: Darius Gray, in "A 54-Year Journey toward Racial Equality in the Mormon Church." Video, 40:19–40:29. The 2018 *Sterling M. McMurrin Lecture on Religion & Culture*, Tanner Humanities Center, published July 9, 2018. Delivered and recorded at the Tanner Humanities Center's "Black, White, & Mormon II Conference," June 29, 2018. Used with permission from the Tanner Humanities Center.

Epigraph, p. 55: Len Ross Hope, in Joseph R. Stuart, "Hope, Len Biography," fourth paragraph. Century of Black Mormons. https://exhibits.lib.utah.edu/s/century-of-black-mormons/page/hope-len. Accessed September 7, 2021 by Alice Faulkner Burch. Courtesy of Century of Black Mormons.

Epigraph, p. 129: Ruffin Bridgeforth, "Ruffin Bridgeforth Autobiography," July 28, 1961, 7–8. Juanita Leone Leavitt Pulsipher Brooks Papers, 1928–1981. J. Willard Marriott Digital Library, University of Utah. https://collections.lib.utah.edu/details?id=1445465&q=Ruffin+Bridgeforth Accessed September 4, 2021, by Alice Faulkner Burch. (Spelling and grammar updated.) Courtesy of Special Collections, J. Willard Marriott Library, University of Utah. Used with permission from Angela Johnson Terry, daughter of Ruffin & Betty Bridgeforth.

Epigraph, p. 171: Freda Lucretia Magee Beaulieu, stake conference talk, January 16, 1982, New Orleans Stake. "Freda Lucretia Magee Beaulieu Biography," Documents, Century of Black Mormons. https://exhibits.lib.utah.edu/s/century-of-black-mormons/page/beaulieu-freda-lucretia-magee#?c=&m=&s=&cv=&xywh=

SOURCES AND CREDITS

-1121%2C0%2C3786%2C1682. Courtesy of Century of Black Mormons.

Abner Leonard Howell photograph, p. 24: "Abner Howell, University of Michigan Football Team, 1902," excerpt from full squad photo. https://quod.lib.umich.edu/b/bhl/x-bl016988/bl016988. Courtesy of University of Michigan Library Digital Collections, Bentley Image Bank, Bentley Historical Library; in the public domain.

Jane Elizabeth Manning James photograph, p. 66: Church of Jesus Christ of Latter-day Saints Church History Library Catalog. Used with permission.

Elizabeth "Bessie" Ritchie Rogers photograph, p. 109: Photographs, Century of Black Mormons. https://exhibits.lib.utah.edu/s/century-of-black-mormons/page/rogers-elizabeth-bessie-ritchie#?c=&m=&s=&cv=&xywh=-358%2C0%2C1106%2C564.

Marie Benjamin Graves photograph, p. 149: Zoomed photo of Marie Graves from a photograph taken of the Oakland Branch members in front of the building, circa 1921 or 1922. Used with permission by Century of Black Mormons.

Samuel Davidson Chambers and Amanda Chambers photograph, p. 173: Photograph of Samuel and Amanda Chambers, 1908; in the public domain.

John Wesley Harmon Jr. photograph, p. 190: Howard Academy Year Book, 1918, page 16; file page 18/68. Courtesy of Digital Library, Howard University. https://dh.howard.edu/cgi/viewcontent.cgi?article=1098&context=bison_yearbooks; in the public domain. Used with permission from Howard University.

All other photos courtesy of the authors.

All poetry original and written specifically for this book by author.